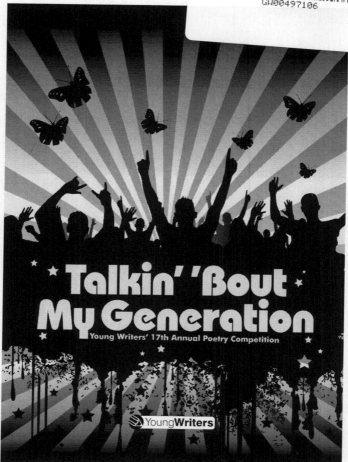

Talkin' 'Bout My Generation

Young Writers' 17th Annual Poetry Competition

YoungWriters

Poems From London
& The Home Counties

Edited by Annabel Cook

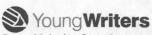 Young**Writers**

First published in Great Britain in 2008 by:
Young Writers
Remus House
Coltsfoot Drive
Peterborough
PE2 9JX
Telephone: 01733 890066
Website: www.youngwriters.co.uk

SB ISBN 978-1 84431 676 2

Foreword

This year, the Young Writers' *Talkin' 'Bout My Generation* competition proudly presents a showcase of the best poetic talent selected from thousands of up-and-coming writers nationwide.

Young Writers was established in 1991 to promote the reading and writing of poetry within schools and to the young of today. Our books nurture and inspire confidence in the ability of young writers and provide a snapshot of poems written in schools and at home by budding poets of the future.

The thought, effort, imagination and hard work put into each poem impressed us all and the task of selecting poems was a difficult but nevertheless enjoyable experience.

We hope you are as pleased as we are with the final selection and that you and your family continue to be entertained with *Talkin' 'Bout My Generation Poems From London & The Home Counties* for many years to come.

Contents

Declan Lockiby 47
Dorrie Britton (13) 48
Alex Adesida (15) 49
Remi Young (14) 50
Naomi Lewis (16) 51
Sean Pursani 52
Brandon Hayward (13) 52
Huy Pham (13) 53
Ashraf Muwawu (13) 54
Tia Elmi (12) 55
William Angwa 55
David Palin 56

Eltham College, Mottingham

Mattias Evans (11) 56
Keerthikan Thirukkumar (12) 57
Toby Fok (14) 57
James Riley (11) 58
Olu Arisekola (13) 59
Lee Partridge (12) 60
Adam Broncz (12) 61
James Morrison (12) 62
William Epps (11) 62
Charlie Murphy (12) 63
Robbie Campbell (13) 63
William Jessop (12) 64
Laurence Hill (12) 65
Michael Jacobs (13) 66
Josh Carty (14) 67
Adam Knox (13) 68
Chris Kruger (13) 69
Alex Robinson (12) 70
Bertie Rowbotham (13) 70
Rory O'Connor Massingham (13) 71
Jamie Phillips (13) 71
Zohaib Siddiqui (14) 72
James Prior (14) 73
David Long (13) 74
Thomas Lavin (14) 75

Alex Jones (14)	76
Stephen Hall (13)	77
Nathan Stables (11)	78
Colby John Dann (12)	79
Cameron Lester (12)	80
Jonathan Hiscock (14)	81
Hamish Hamilton (13)	82
Thomas Michael Ian Wilson (14)	83
Matthew Burgess (13)	84
Harrison Wilson (12)	85
Aman Gupta (11)	86
Sebastian Wiseman (13)	87

JFS School, Harrow

Tomer Banai (12)	87
Emily Curtis (11)	88
Asal Reyhanian (11)	89
Michael Simons (12)	90
Kelli Wegoda (11)	91
Andrew Roth (11)	92
Sophie Corper (11)	93
Jonathan Richards (12)	94
Charlotte Kaye (11)	95
Fiona Bleetman (12)	96
Daniella Myers (11)	97
Ariella Kramer (11)	98
Josh Gurvitz (11)	99
Georgia Mooney (12)	100
Katie Barker (12)	100
Jack Shlomi (12)	101
Joseph Eskenazy (12)	101
Sarah Shamia (12)	102
David Schmidt (11)	103
Idan Levy (12)	104
James Crown (12)	104
Sharon Bamberg (12)	105
Kelly Levy (12)	105
Nicholas Bloch (12)	106
Ella Bernie (11)	107

The Poems

Why?

Why should I be the hero?
Let someone else fight and stand up for what they think is right.
Why should I watch people begging for their lives?
Gives me no pleasure to watch them die.
Why should I serve this country?
When all they want is death and misery.
Why should I hold this gun?
You do it - if you think it's fun
Would you cry?
If a bullet were to hit me
Would you remember my face?
This time next week.
And now I'm haunted by this misery
Blood on my hands - there's no way I can be free
An eternal agony
I see a soldier's heart bring ripped in two
This is the honest truth
So block your ears
Shield the truth
Keep on believing the lie
Just know nothing is fine.

Lanya Kawa (14)

How Solemn Are These White Graves Of Flanders

How solemn are these white graves of Flanders!
These teeth whose roots reach down to death's core
Where dead bodies lie
In madness and torment
They are slaves to war's memory
Planted in Hell's mouth from which there is no escape,
Now I am alone,
Facing this dead army -
Though it is alive because we think it victorious,
But how wrong we are!
They lament in their slumber
And long for revenge,
The sky is bleak
And the graves line the horizon -
How solemn are these white graves of Flanders!

Sophie de Beistegui (14)

Reality

All around us are memorable faces
Worn down places,
But unlike you
I observe a dissimilar place
A dissimilar world,
I see lies, laughs, love
Everyone acts differently,
To different people
In different ways,
We are living in a fake world
Fake lives, fake everything,
People are dying
Because of carelessness,
Selfish individuals,
Why is our world
Constantly brutal?

Jade Pickett (13)
Bishopshalt School, Uxbridge

Kids These Days

They're talking about my generation . . .
They don't think,
They just hang out on street corners having a drink,
They spit,
They swear,
They really don't care.
They have no respect for us
And look at what they wear.
I think you've got the message about kids today,
A few are fine, but most should go away.

I'm talking for my generation . . .
I am a kid, I'm nearly a teen,
I don't spit,
I don't swear (much)
And I'm really quite clean.
I respect the older generation for what they have done,
For fighting in wars, for facing the gun.
But they show no respect,
They're killing our planet
And don't ask themselves why,
They continue to send poison into the sky.

Us kids of all races, religions and friends,
Will protect the planet to the very end,
So generations for years to come,
Can still love the world 'cause of what we've done.

Matthew Schlachter (11)
Bishopshalt School, Uxbridge

Unrealistic Statistic

Call me one, call him two,
But then again, it's not up to you
In a society, where we are all treated as numbers
Sometimes my brain starts to wonder
If I'm considered anything more than just a statistic
But as the future generation, let us be optimistic

Let's believe one person *can* really make a change
Not just be another capitalistic slave
Have a system where you can succeed, in a meritocratic society
And not affected by your wealth, colour, gender, but personality

Let's be proud that we are all complex, unique human beings
Not just numbers on a graph the government are seeing
Testing us from the day we are born
Don't they realise that the mind can flourish
When it's not forced to conform

Let's not allow our generation to simply be typecast
We can write the script, have a legacy that will last
The media are unwilling to show both sides
That young people are not perfect, but we also contribute to life

So, let's live life through meaning and what we feel
Wish to be treated like we're actually real
Because we can all be the greatest in the future to come
And the only statistic I want to see?
That there are none . . .

Martin Barker (17)
Bishopshalt School, Uxbridge

I'm Special

When I'm pitied,
It causes me pain.
When I'm left out,
I feel consciously lame.
Why can't they see,
That I am special?

I can read and write,
Just as they do.
But even bright
And I play the flute!
The best paralympist,
In my school.
Understanding student,
Not a fool.
Why can't they see,
That I'm special?

Making friends,
I'm good at.
I've a Mum, Dad
And I live in a flat.
Cooking food,
Is my speciality.
Painting pictures,
Is a personality.
But still . . .
Why can't they see,
That I'm special?

Ashorya Gurung (12)
Bishopshalt School, Uxbridge

Do You Think Of Others?

Do you think
Of the people around you?
Or do you just wonder
Why the sky is blue?

Do you prefer
To share with your friend?
Or are you selfish
And don't lend?

Do you help
Those in need?
Or are you a bystander
And miss a good deed?

If you think of others,
Others will think of you,
Share your thoughts and feelings
And no one will think of you as, who?

Distribute to the poor,
So that they think of you,
That there are people who care about others
And can at least donate a shoe.

So, the moral of this poem is,
To look around everywhere,
Give a hand to make the world better
And spread the word of happiness and care!

Karan Sethi (12)
Bishopshalt School, Uxbridge

It All Carried On . . .

I always tried to reach out as far as I could,
But never did I touch the line.
I worked hard, tried to achieve high,
Yet, never did I seem to shine.

I did everything I could to make my parents proud,
Working harder, working faster,
I did my best, my very best,
Yet, always all I'd hear was laughter.

In my heart, I knew it couldn't be done,
Although I pushed so much,
I found my way through, now and again
And somewhere, I'd lose my clutch.

The shouting and screaming, I'd hear all the time,
Never seemed to matter on the outside,
Nobody knew the inside though,
I wanted to run and hide.

Years of hassle, I was told to ignore
And for so long, I did just that.
I didn't scream, shout or cry at night,
But always, alone I sat.

The people around me would say so much,
All I could do was ignore.
I listened to them all day long,
Until I could take it no more.

I cried so much, again and again,
Unable to handle it all.
The years of pain and misery,
From people, big and small.

The night went by and the next day came,
But nobody seemed to care,
It all carried on, just like before,
For me, no one was really there . . .

Sana Qureshi (16)
Bishopshalt School, Uxbridge

Alien

You need me,
Which makes me seethe.
I get sick,
You wait to breathe.

An unwanted guest,
Existing, powerless . . . small.
It's my body, your bed,
Scrunched up in a ball.

I ignore everything,
You kick barriers wafer thin.
Reminding me you're still here,
Without diplomacy or limb.

No secrets in our circle,
You caused such a fuss.
Clasping at my family chain,
No bond between us.

I could wrap you in paper,
Pale pink or baby blue.
Given away, like a gift,
Deprived of everything you do.

A blemish they remove,
Cut away from inside.
No chance to open your eyes,
Before you lived, you died.

The crimson agony of birth,
Vice-like, you won't let go.
Clinging fiercely to me,
I scream out, 'No!'

This is more than I can take,
The Product of one mistake.

Penny Chate (17)
Bishopshalt School, Uxbridge

I Am Homeless

My name is Tom, I am 12 years old
I live in a box where my feet are cold
All I have to eat in a day, is a mould apple and a cup of smelly milk
And all I do for fun, is sit in the rain, full of pain
I might as well be dead
I am already dead to the world
At daytime, I hide from the cops
Because they will put me in a foster home
I hate them
I went to one last year
I ran away, thank God
The only thing I have ever owned
Is a bear named Dear the Dinimight
I am homeless.

Tom Costello (12)
Brampton Manor School, East Ham

The Living Classroom!

The teacher's gone
The door is closed
Out come the pencils from their pot
The pens all follow without a doubt
The rubbers jump onto the table
Then come the books, they're all fables
Their playtime is nearly over
They all jump back into their places
The teacher's come back
And look at their faces!

Amy Field (11)
Brampton Manor School, East Ham

Be A Leader, Not A Follower

Don't be a follower, be a leader
Show your people the way
Help them become stronger, day by day
If you are a follower, you are a sheep
If you are a leader, you are like a roaring lion
Ready to defend your people, even the poor.

Be as royal as a king
And as proud as a knight
And if you are in school, show your friends
It is not cool to act a fool
Be like the great leaders from the past
Like Martin Luther King and Nelson Mandela
Let the world remember your memory, forever.

Shingirayi Mararike (12)
Brampton Manor School, East Ham

I Support Manchester United

I support Manchester Unite
I am a fan of Rooney
I don't support West Ham
I am not a maniac loony
I am very good at football
Whatever I do, I pull up my socks
And stand up tall
Yes, yes, it's me, TK
I'll never lose in a relay.

Thamana Khanom (12)
Brampton Manor School, East Ham

As . . .

As red as a juicy red tomato
As green as the greenest green broccoli
As yellow spotted as a yellow spotted lizard
As sweet as an ice cream in the summer
As juicy as a freshly made milkshake
As hard as a pineapple
As crunchy as a packet of crisps
As bumpy as the bumpiest road you have ever seen
As hairy as a fully-grown hairy man
As soft as a pillow
As juicy as a fully-grown fruit
Here, take it from my hand.

Ivan Dimitrov (12)
Brampton Manor School, East Ham

Mother's Day

Mothers are far much better than diamonds and rubies
She can take care of us
She cooks and cleans
And she takes good care of us when we are sick
I don't know about your mum
But my mum's an angel
She's more than just a mum
She's my best friend!

Esther Asabi (12)
Brampton Manor School, East Ham

Cute Fruit

My favourite fruit is banana
So I eat one when I can
They taste real good and look so cute
All dressed up in a yellow suit.

Who makes these bananas anyway?
They do a good job, I must say
Don't know exactly how they seal them
I think about it when I peel them.

Yellow, yellow as a pillow
Five in a pack
Where would you find them?
I know, in a sack
As sweet and cute as they are
They can't run very far.

Frankie Taylor (11)
Brampton Manor School, East Ham

School

I hate school
It isn't cool
I get detention
In that I do comprehension
The teachers are weird
That's the only thing I feared
I get all the boring lessons
And some exhausting fitness sessions.

Muhammad Osama (12)
Brampton Manor School, East Ham

Star Bright, Star Light

Star bright, star light
The first star I see tonight
I wish I may, I wish I might
Have the wish I wish tonight.

When you see the star tonight
It's called a sun
And when you wish
It sparkles through your eyes.

Star bright, star light
The first star I see tonight
I wish I may, I wish I might
Have the wish I wish tonight.

Do you wish for something big?
Do you wish for something small?
It might come true
But it might not.

Star bright, star light
The first star I see tonight
I wish I may, I wish I might
Have the wish I wish tonight.

Jhanara Begum (11)
Brampton Manor School, East Ham

The Strawberry Poem

Strawberries are juicy
Strawberries are red
Strawberries are big
I love strawberries
They're really, really juicy
I love strawberries
They're really, really lovely
I just love strawberries!

Samantha Newberry (11)
Brampton Manor School, East Ham

Pain

I hear them shouting,
I hear them fighting,
Into my heart they are smiting.

I don't know what to do,
Or what to say,
I see their happiness slipping away.

I peek through the door
And my head is tilted,
Their flower of love has now wilted.

I look at them fighting
And I cry and cry,
As I see their marriage go awry.

It's over, they've stopped,
I sit there and stare in shock,
The people I know, they mock, they mock.

The pain is too much,
The pain is too great,
I pack my bags and I run away.

I don't know where I'm going,
But I don't care,
As long as anger and hatred aren't there.

I'm in social care now,
But it's so much more fun,
Here anger and hatred never comes,
It never comes.

Shifa Patel (12)
Brampton Manor School, East Ham

Back To School

Dear students, the summer has ended,
The school year, at last, has begun,
But this year is totally different,
We're going to only have fun.

We won't study any mathematics
And recess will last all day long,
Instead of the pledge of allegiance,
We'll belt out a rock and roll song.

We'll only play games in the classroom,
You're welcome to bring in your own toys,
It's OK to run in the hallways,
It's great if you make lots of noise.

Your video games are your homework,
You'll have to watch lots of TV,
For field trips we'll go to the movies
And give away candy for free.

Rumika Roy (12)
Brampton Manor School, East Ham

School Poem

I go to school
And be so cool,
I have so many lessons
And get so tired,
Most teachers should get fired,
Every day I wake up so drowsy,
All the men teachers wear blouses,
Finally the last bus goes,
Home sweet home.

Arun Singh Kahlon (12)
Cranford Community College, Hounslow

Eyewitness

I am an eyewitness that you cannot feel or hear
For years you have been trying to touch me
Yet I watch your every move
From when you wake up in the morning
To when you go to sleep at night
I have seen every catastrophe the Earth has ever dealt with
I see the planets and the stars
And I watch the comets pass the Earth
As I twist and turn
Yet you still carry on polluting me
I just want to let you know
I feel the heat and the cold
And from now on
I'm going to sit back and watch the future unfold.

Joel Tyrell-Pinnock (12)
Cranford Community College, Hounslow

If You Had A Wish

If you could wish for anything,
What in the whole world would it be?
A bike? A PC? Or a game console?
What will be your one wish?
Will you wish for a million pounds?
You might just wish a mansion with a pool,
That is as big as a whole school,
Or you might wish for a lot of toys,
Might even be a private jet,
The pilot's flying you anywhere at anytime,
These are wishes you might make,
Or wish for lots more wishes,
To make them all.

Navroj Singh (12)
Cranford Community College, Hounslow

What Is A Good Friend?

A A good friend should agree
That we are all different

B A good friend should believe
In you

C A good friend should always
Care for you

D A good friend should
Defend you

E A good friend should
Encourage you

F A good friend should
Always be friendly to you

G A good friend should
Be generous to you

H A good friend should
Help you

I A good friend should
Interfere to help you with problems

J A good friend should
Give you justice

K A good friend should
Always be kind to you

L A good friend should
Never lie to you

M A good friend should
Never be mean to you

N A good friend should
Not be nasty to you

O A good friend should
Obey you

P A good friend should
Persuade you

Q A good friend should
Be quiet when you don't want to talk

R A good friend should
Respect you

S A good friend should
Keep you safe

T A good friend should
  Be trustworthy
U A good friend should
  Not be unpleasant
V A good friend should
  Not vandalise your things
W A good friend should
  Always wait for you
X A good friend should
  Expect the best
Y A good friend should not
  Yawn when you are talking
Z A good friend should never
  Zigzag on you
  Like saying they are your friend
  When they're really not.

Sara Brahimi (12)
Cranford Community College, Hounslow

Weather

The sun is bright
The wind is strong
The rain is wet
The fog has gone
Weather
The clouds open
Lightning flashes
Hail falls
Thunder crashes
Weather
Play in the snow
Skate on ice
All kinds of weather
Can be nice
Weather!

Matthew James (12)
Cranford Community College, Hounslow

I Love You, Boy

I love you more than you can see
You make me feel so happy,
I love you, boy, you're one of a kind
I want you to know, you will always be mine.

My boyfriend's eyes are deeper than the sea
He always tells me that he loves me,
He hugs me tight and never lets go
But when he is ready, he will let go slow.

I love you more than you can see
You make me feel so happy,
I love you, boy, you're one of a kind,
I want you to know, you will always be mine.

My boyfriend has the cutest smile
He makes me think I am worthwhile,
He will always say, 'I love you'
I will reply, 'I love you too.'

I love you more than you can see
You make me feel so happy,
I love you, boy, you are one of a kind,
I want you to know, you will always be mine.

Rhiane Stiff (12)
Cranford Community College, Hounslow

Eyewitness

A camera is an eyewitness
When you take pictures
It can show proof
It can see what is happening, when it happens
Cameras can see everything.

I am little and I can see everything
I can take pictures of everything
People can smash me
I can still know what I have seen
I am the most clever eyewitness.

I am the trouble of everyone
People can't take that I have all the proof
If only I could talk
I would go to the police station by walking
I would tell them everything.

I am the camera
The most deadly eyewitness
No one can see
What I can see
That will never change
That is the truth.

Aakash Mishra (11)
Cranford Community College, Hounslow

Luxury Love

My love, your eyes are deeper than the deepest sea,
When I look into your eyes
I know you're the one and the only one
When I touch your cherry-red lips
I faint and think of your bendy hips
When I put my chin under your skin
I smell a wonderful strawberry aroma
When I think of you
My heart sinks into you
I love you with all my heart
And I hope you know that too
I hope our love lasts forever
Because, no matter what
You'll always be with me
Forever and ever.

Humzah Saeed (12)
Cranford Community College, Hounslow

Blind As A Bat

I wake up every morning,
Not knowing where I am,
I look outside the window
And wonder what's going on.
I always walk around the house,
Observing my every move,
I wonder what I would be,
If I could just see.
Would I be a footballer
Or maybe a boxer
Or even a company advisor?
I wonder, I wonder.
So, I hope you know who I am,
A blind, old, withered man
And my name is . . .

Amit Mehmi (11)
Cranford Community College, Hounslow

Looking For God

Looking around for God, was I,
I looked down in the sea
And I looked up in the sky,
I couldn't find His eyes or His head,
I couldn't find His mouth or His legs,
But I could feel Him by my side.

I looked to the right . . . but still no clue,
I looked to the left . . . but still no sight.

I looked up
And I looked down,
But there was no such evidence,
Of God being there.

I looked to the right . . . but still no clue,
I looked to the left . . . but still no sight.

I keep praying to see such sight of You, God,
Something I am not able to sleep all night,
I imagine You in my dreams . . . in my dreams,
I imagine You in my heart . . . in my heart,
I hear my echoes saying, 'Where are You, God?'
I don't know if I chose the right time to start.

I looked to the right . . . but still no clue,
I looked to the left . . . but still no sight.

Why do you keep testing me, God?
Each time I feel lost and alone,
You put my faith to another test,
I thought deep down and realised something special,
That God is in my family,
God is in my teachers
And God is in my friends.
God bless everyone!

Neeha Kapoor (12)
Cranford Community College, Hounslow

On The Day I Was Born

On the day that I was born,
My father was so proud,
No other baby in the crib
Could scream and cry as loud.

No other baby kicked
Its covers to the nursery floor,
No other baby drank its milk,
Then yelled, 'I want some more!'

And when I messed my diapers,
Nurses rang the fire bell,
The firemen with hoses,
Would spray the nursery well.

I would have been so boring,
So quiet and well-bred,
If the clumsy doctor,
Hadn't dropped me on my head!

Manjinder Kang (12)
Cranford Community College, Hounslow

Colours

Red is like a burning flame
Red is like a boring game
Blue is like a wavy sea
Blue is like the sky facing me
Green is like the wonderful grass
Green is like a car rushing past
Orange is like the sun settling down
Orange is the colour of a rushing town
Black is the colour of lightning
Black is the colour of two cats fighting
Pink is the colour of fresh roses
Pink is like a catwalk of poses
Yellow is the colour of honey
Yellow is like the colour of the sky when it's sunny
Peach is like the colour of a beach
Peach is the colour of stars out of reach
Brown is the colour of a bear
Brown is the colour of my hair
White is like a soft cloud
White is like a child screaming out loud.

Davina Thiara (12)
Cranford Community College, Hounslow

The Real World

A shadow that lies
On half of the world
All these negative signs
Pointing the wrong way,
Darkness crawling around
A tiny whisper says
That all the happiness is gone
But no sound.

I look left . . . no smiles
I look right . . . no smiles,

Fading away
Is the light
Yet the darkness
Stays in sight,
A crime committed
Every single second
Screams and cries
I reckon.

I look left . . . no smiles
I look right . . . no smiles,

Repeating the word 'hate'
Makes me quiver
And repeating the word 'evil'
Makes me shiver,
Finding a way
Out of this world
But no escape
Can be heard or told.

I look left . . . no smiles
I look right . . . no smiles.

Manisha Bangar (12)
Cranford Community College, Hounslow

Feelings!

Happy
Joyful
Pleased
And glad.

Annoyed
Frustrated
Upset
And sad.

Depressed
Unhappy
When I'm feeling bad.

Alone
Abandoned
Neglected
And scared.

Strong
Aggressive
Thoughts
And braveness.

Hurt
Grieve
Pain
The tears.

We all have feelings, me and you
Sometimes we're happy, sometimes we're blue
And at some point we're all excited
So let's make our feelings feel invited!

Babita Sidhu (12)
Cranford Community College, Hounslow

Untitled

Were you there at my birth?
In the same room while I was being conceived?

Were you there when I took my first steps?
Please tell me, I'm feeling intrigued.

Were you there when I mentioned my very first word?
Could it have been your name?

Were you there when I started nursery school
And won the noughts and crosses game?

Where you there when I wrote my very first story
A special day in Year 2?

Were you there when I started secondary school?
I wanted to be with you.

Were you there last Friday at seven o'clock
On the cold street of London
Where a guy pulled up in a black car
And shot me all of a sudden?

Michael Kwakye
Crofton School, London

Untitled

My generation is in frustration
Teens walk around in devastation
The atmosphere makes you feel a sensation
A sensation of violation
Why can't we all live in civilisation?
My nation is in botheration
Immigration has tortured my generation
All this discrimination has caused global segregation
I walk looking down, as I face humiliation.

Venesa Morris
Crofton School, London

My Generation

M y generation is growing up so quickly
Y et we have no self-control

G uns, knives, murders
E veryone is affected
N o one feels safe on the streets
E veryone should be treated the same
R aces, there are so many races
A nd people need to accept this
T hey need to learn that
I t needs to change
O r else there will be no more of our generation left
N ever let this happen, please.

Jack Pollard (13)
Crofton School, London

Untitled

Talking 'bout my generation
Isn't very hard
From drugs to crime
And crime to discrimination
The streets aren't safe
Danger around every corner
Why is it happening?

Terrorism is a creeping shadow
Clouding our lives
People making choices
Not thinking it's fair
This is my generation
But I don't think you understand
I love it.

Yasir Mushtaq
Crofton School, London

Talkin' 'Bout My Generation

T he knife and gun crime rate is really high
A nd everyone around here is tellin'
L ies
K ids and teens
I nto stuff they shouldn't, which
N ever could be good

B ad websites help kids
O n their way to the gutter
U nder all the badness inside
T hey are only kids after all

M ore and more terrorism is about
Y oung kids dying everywhere

G hanaian and Brazilian kids are dying from poverty
E ngland is much better off
N ever in this country have I seen people stop and think
E ven higher goes the teenage pregnancy
R ate
A nd
T hey think it's the girls to blame
I n school, kids are not learning
O n and on, will it
N ever *stop!*

Kieran Loughery
Crofton School, London

Talkin' 'Bout My Generation

T oday there is so much crime
A ll the time, people getting killed
L ies make sure no one ever gets caught
K ids now regarded as thugs
I n England
N o one thinks they're safe

B ut what about people that are not involved
O h, if only they got recognised
U nder all of this crime
T here must be so many good citizens out there, but that's

M y generation for you
Y es, it's not a great place to be

G etting scared every night
E nding many lives, there are violent thugs, but why do they
N ever get caught?
E verybody wants these thugs to be caught, but the police never
R ealise how much crime means to
A ll the citizens, so
T herefore, crime doesn't get noticed as much anymore
I n this world
O bviously
N o one feels safe.

Darren Ash (12)
Crofton School, London

Talkin' 'Bout Your Generation

Who is the future? What are they like?
Are they like Yasir, shiny and bright?
Are they like Tristan, having a think?
Are they like Pauline, looks good in pink?
Are they like Crystal, serious and deep?
Or even like Ken, always half asleep . . .
What about Andre sat in the middle?
Or Michael who's always got something to twiddle.
Who are the thinkers? What are their thoughts?
Will they remember the things they've been taught?
What of Vanessa, as sharp as a pin?
Or Georgie who babbles and never gives in?
Then there is Martin (reading again)
And Elyon and Charmaine exercising their brains.
Aishat is chatting and working her smile
Funda's done her best piece of work in a while
Arshia's still talking and making *more* noise
Jack raises an eyebrow and glares at the boys
Kieran is fidgeting, heads for the door
Darren works quietly, who could want more?
Ahleeyah and Ashawnie are dreaming of shoes . . .
Aidan's perfecting his broken leg moves
Sharisse isn't smiling, she's our Mona Lisa
Conroy is dreaming of TV and pizza
Finally, Kingsley, ready and willing
And Maryam, joined us for a new beginning
The future is theirs, they build our nation
Talkin' 'bout their generation.

Annie Hadley-Stone
Crofton School, London

Untitled

Why do drugs?
It won't get you anywhere
Young people think it is cool to smoke
Well, let me tell you it's not
People dying as young teenagers
Little babies dying because their parents smoke
Children walking on the road
Then a car comes and hits them
Because they don't think
People think because they have sex, they might have HIV
Gangs shooting kids
Kids run for their lives
Is this meant to be cool?
Let me tell you, it's not!
Want to know why?
Because you will never make it.

Kingsley Fajuyigbe
Crofton School, London

Teen Trouble: Is It Safe . . . Anymore?

I walk outside my house,
Oh no, not again.
I hear a scream and I see people
Running away.
Dressed in black, they push me back
And make me feel unsafe.

I am too frightened to do anything
I find courage to call the police.
This is the third time this year,
I don't dare go around the corner.

Charlotte Mealings (12)
Crown Woods School, London

Teenage Life

They walk the streets,
Misunderstood,
People flee,
From their hoods.

People think,
They are bad,
But really,
They're just deeply sad.

They've got nowhere to go,
So they stay on the streets,
Starting fights and abusing drugs,
They finally gain the attention they gave.

Give them a chance,
Trust them for once,
Make them safe,
Don't feed them sweets,
Show them respect
And they'll show you peace.

Amirah Adekunle (12)
Crown Woods School, London

The World Is Dying

The ice is melting
And the sea is rising.
The sea is hot
And the heat is rising.
People don't know,
But the world is dying.

We drive around in big, fancy cars
And watch TV and turn on lights,
Most don't know what's going on,
But all I know is the world is dying.

Buildings stand there, tall and high,
Looking down on me.
Smoke comes out from the top,
Blowing in the air,
Making the sun get hot.
I don't know why this happens,
But all I know is the world is dying.

Adam Green (12)
Crown Woods School, London

Trouble

I walk out my house, no longer am I safe,
I sense danger coming my way,
I see violence, I hear mothers crying
From another dying son.
A group of boys, dressed in black,
Ready to attack,
Can they not see the violence?
Can they hear more mothers crying?
There they are, with knives, hoping that they won't have to fight,
They don't have to do it, they have a choice.
Now I stand here, carrying a knife,
I hope that I will not have to fight,
But I have to, to keep me safe,
Or I will feel unsafe.
But it's not just me, it happens everywhere,
We want to stop it,
It must happen now
Or I will still see violence
And I will still hear more mothers crying.

Alisha Artry (12)
Crown Woods School, London

Teenagers

Terrorism
Ealing
MurdEr
SweariNg
VAndalism
Graffiti
WEapons
CRimes
Shoplifting

These are the thoughts that people think of
When they see teenagers on the street . . .

Anita Dhani (12)
Crown Woods School, London

Nightmare World

I stand outside the safety of my home,
A gang of dark figures approach,
I turn and sprint as fast as I can,
Until I find a place to hide,
But I see a young boy oblivious to the gang,
I yell to him at the top of my lungs,
But he can't hear me,
I hear a sharp scream . . . then a gunshot . . .
Then a silence so untrue.

Another innocent child has been killed for no reason at all,
His mother is crying, her head in her hands;
She has no one left to hold,
Her husband was killed for standing up for what he believed in
And was beaten with a hammer,
Her daughter died at birth, but the gunman won't know that,
For to him, it's just another boy who got in the way.

Suddenly, a hand on my shoulder,
A shadow hangs over me,
I scream, but a foot kicks my ribs,
Another kicks my face,
I lay helpless on the floor with a gun to my head,
I dare not say a word,
For if I do, I fear that my life will be taken,
Just like the boy before,
The unknown hand pulls the trigger,
My life flashes before my eyes . . .

Libby Southwell (12)
Crown Woods School, London

Multicultural England

I walk down the high street and see so many different faces.
So many different colours and kinds, they vary from so many places.
I hear many sounds,
Many languages of which I am not familiar.

Many different smells,
From which country I cannot tell.
Many churches, mosques and temples,
Religious traditions.

I eat many foods,
Chinese, Indian and Jamaican.
I have many friends from all over the globe,
From numerous places I can only dream of going to.
They wear many clothes, like scarves, robes and suits.
But I respect them because they stay true to their roots.

Nathan King (15) & Sverrir Kristinsson (14)
Deptford Green School, New Cross

Inside

Tell me where your memories rest
Tell me where you're broken-hearted,
Happy or feeling kinda depressed.
Where the good things are
And where future ones go . . .
The bad things we just can't forget,
The sorrows we all know.
Things that make us suffer,
Can be so different, yet the same.
Sometimes our problems can help us . . .
And sometimes drive us insane.
If you're feeling down,
Look inside this place
And block the problems out . . .
Focus on the best.

Kat Petrovic
Deptford Green School, New Cross

Feeling Alone . . . But People Are Around

Feeling alone, but people are around,
I don't know why,
Just a quiet sound,
Sometimes it makes me want to frown,
Even though everyone is there,
But sometimes I just feel like sitting there - to stare,
I love all my friends; I don't know why I feel this way,
Someone tell me, please,
I think about it every day,
Sometimes it just makes my heart freeze,
Feeling alone, even though there are people around,
Please come, talk to me, I'm feeling down.

Nicolle Cross
Deptford Green School, New Cross

If Love . . . ?

If love is blind
Why can I see you?
If love is kind
Why do I feel blue?
If love is happy
Why am I sad?

If love is pure
Why don't I trust you?
If love has a cure
What should I do?
If our love has died
Why are we still together?

Molly Florey (15)
Deptford Green School, New Cross

For Rebecca

(From Julius Lester's 'Basketball Game')

Oh, Rebecca, Rebecca, Rebecca,
I love you,
I've had feelings for you since the day we met.
There is something though, I do regret,
We did not spend enough time together,
But you're the only one I could be with forever.
I don't think this is the same for you,
As I might be your number 222.
I don't really care how you spend your time,
I love you: I want you to be mine.
The time you blanked me, really stayed in my heart,
At that time, I thought we would fall apart.
To know that you weren't just next door,
Made me almost drop to the floor.
I don't care what they say,
I'm in love with you,
Just don't push me away.
You don't know the truth,
I know how I feel about you now,
If we could turn back time,
You'd be mine.

Truyen Le (14)
Deptford Green School, New Cross

The Stages Of Life

Many people want to know what life is all about
And what is the point of living,
Life is a challenge,
The goal is to live as much as possible
And sometimes to create another life.
More and more competitors,
Come into this competition
And some can't cope and fade away,
For example,
The little ones can't cope,
Without someone to help them,
They need to be educated,
Fed, bathed and loved,
But as they get older, they depend less on others,
They fade away from the people they love,
But get more involved with the world
And that's what makes them successful,
To try new things
And to be happy with themselves,
The prize is all the memories,
Put together,
Into bundles of joy.

Charlotte Harris
Deptford Green School, New Cross

How I Feel

It's amazing how I feel when I'm around you,
How my heart pounds when you come into a room.
I look at you and think, *my God! How lovely!*
And everything I am bursts into bloom.

I feel as though you must, you must be mine,
Not as a possession, but as a goal,
Something almost unimaginable,
The free devotion of another soul.

As though I were about to enter Heaven,
Or just within the hour condemned to die,
My mind with one fierce thought, keeps running over,
With you and only you, the reason why.

Jamie Hollamby
Deptford Green School, New Cross

The Perfect Crime

I look at you, you look at me,
My heart jumps, but nobody sees.
I just wanna hold your hand in mine,
But I don't wanna hide this time.
It's concealing, not revealing,
No more keeping inside,
Sick of this hiding,
I plead guilty.
Could it be destiny?
Were you really made for me?
We committed the perfect crime,
I stole your heart and you stole mine.
My mind is stressing,
The truth is undressing.
All this pretending,
These lies are ending,
I plead guilty.

Katie Mac
Deptford Green School, New Cross

Love, Disguised

I walk on stage,
Performing reality.
I stare at his eyes,
He looks on the floor.

He brushes his fingers through my hair
And twirls it.
I lay with my eyes closed,
Heart pounding, like poison
Swimming through my veins.

He kisses me on my forehead,
He says a few words
And pulls out a shiny warhead
And the words form into tears.

An ear-splitting blast disperses from the shiny object,
He lies on the floor.
I wake up, at last
And seek for the opening door.

I see no way out of this,
The only way is to go with him.
I hunt for the thing that took him away
And placed it on my heart.

I pull the trigger,
I die.

Audience claps and curtain closes,
I stepped out of the shoes I wore.
But he didn't,
He stayed on the floor.

Sleepy.

We tried to wake him up
And realised,
This was no play.

He took the role of Romeo
And Romeo took him away.

Alice Tu (14)
Deptford Green School, New Cross

Love And Hate

Love
Here on my knees,
Clinging to your hand,
Chanting my love and pleas,
'Let's go away, somewhere not too grand.'

When you feel unsure,
Stay in my arms,
My heart's an open door,
In need of your charms.

Here we sit,
Alone and scared,
Few candles lit,
Our hearts now flared.

Hate
Anger exploding in my skull,
Her face torments my eyes,
Poisoning my very soul,
Only to smile,
When she lays down and dies.

She lays asleep,
Breathing ever slowly,
Thrusted deep
Her face turning ghostly.

Lauren Tripp
Deptford Green School, New Cross

Love And Hate

Love
It's like a dream
Thinking about the shadow men
Of an expressed love train. It hits me
While chasing the meaning of love
I slowly, patiently, approach the dismantled train,
I awaken, taking time to take a breath.
The picture seems me fading and dull
It burns in the dark sky
Suddenly, realising she's my lover.

Hate
It started in the hair salon
Doing what girls do . . .
Dressing up
The conversation continued
Hatred of my worst enemy
She stole something of mine
Very precious, sweet and kind
She spoilt my life by taking it
She can have it
I'm over him!

Michaela St John
Deptford Green School, New Cross

Crime

Why is there so much crime on the news?
You choose,
You never win,
Only lose.

Big men getting drunk on booze,
People robbing banks,
Acting like fools.

Men blowing their fuse,
Children being abused,
Women being raped and used.

Homicide,
Genocide,
Put all of them aside.

Knife crime,
Gun crime,
Does it have to happen
All of the time?

Gregory Eyebi-Kadock (13)
Deptford Green School, New Cross

Why?

Why separate ourselves because of colour?
Things like this make us hurt each other
Could be a gun, maybe a knife
Being racist is not worth your life
There is no difference, just our race of skin
We all need to see the person within
Think before you act, because racism can hurt
It can hurt you and the ones you love
It's not worth it . . .

Tyra Manning-Johnson (13)
Deptford Green School, New Cross

Venice

Past the slow-flowing rivers
And the heavily decorated shops,
Water runs instead of roads,
My reflection everywhere -
City of mirrors.

The sun, hotter and brighter
Than ever, a stunning red cherry
In the blue, blue sky,
Birds dip in and out of
The milky clouds.

Through the city I stroll,
My journey through
The city of roads that
Reflect my face, in
This city of mirrors -
Venice.

Maya Williams (12)
Deptford Green School, New Cross

Racism

Racism has not yet left the world
Why is it still here?
Why is it still around?
Black, white, mixed race, Oriental, Indian
Why does it matter?
Why does the colour of your skin play such a part?
It can really hurt someone in their heart
Why is it still here?
Why is it still around?

Declan Lockiby
Deptford Green School, New Cross

Time To Break Out

I tried to change it, put it right
Joined the ANC
So many leaflet bombs
Hard to keep control

Police came to my house
Found the keys
Keys to my secret garage
Leaflet bombs hidden inside

Sent to jail for twelve years
A lot of time to think
I wanted out
But I had twelve years to wait

Decided to escape
On my own at first
Making the first key
Took three months

People joined in
Many keys were made
People pulled out
Only three of us tried

Opening the six doors was easy
Door seven was tricky
We hadn't make a key
Luckily, another worked

Tricked the warden
Office left empty
Went in, pressed the button
Opened electric door eight

We came to door nine
No key worked!
Break it down?
Too much noise?

Chipped off wood by handle
Broke the lock
It opened!
We weren't free yet

Had to go to Swaziland
To be free
One went one way
Two stuck together

We walked a long time
We caught a lift
The man let us in
We were on our way

We said thanks
We walked and walked
We thought we were far
We slept when walking

We crossed the border
But we didn't know
We asked a girl
We were in Swaziland

Freedom!

Dorrie Britton (13)
Deptford Green School, New Cross

Freedom

Freedom is the right to choose
Freedom is swimming in a pool
Freedom is the food we eat
Freedom is the thing we drink
Freedom is the air we breathe
Freedom is like nice smelling cheese
Freedom is the game we play
Freedom is the place we stay
Freedom is the right to give
Freedom is the life we live.

Alex Adesida (15)
Deptford Green School, New Cross

Street Corner

At the street corner
9.00am downtown New York,
A pile of rags in the doorway
With a homeless man hidden within
Sitting on a newspaper
Staring into the eyes of passers-by

He catches the eye of a man
The man in a three-piece linen suit
With short, styled, dark brown hair
Carrying a jet-black briefcase

The homeless man
Tired from his sleepless night
Grimy and unhygienic
Holds out a piece of cardboard
Pleading for change

Both men, roughly the same age
Gaze at each other for a split second
Holding both close together
As if everything were possible.

Remi Young (14)
Deptford Green School, New Cross

Steps

The entrance of a corner shop
Steps
That seems easy enough to get up
When you have two legs in perfect working order
Just about to go in
Then you see
A middle-aged man in a wheelchair
You feel sympathetic
How did that happen? You think to yourself
You see the look of distress on his face
As he approaches the shop
Just a few *steps* for you
But they're a headache for him
You decide to help him
You touch the cold rubber of the handles on his wheelchair
You've just been struck by lightning
The currents of electricity go through you
You then realise how grateful you should be for just
Being able to walk up a few
Steps.

Naomi Lewis (16)
Deptford Green School, New Cross

Opposite Worlds

They stare and gaze
At this opposite world,
Nothing matters now.
Their hopes seem shattered
As their dreams turn to nightmares,
For nothing will end well.

This world they see is full
Of happiness and love,
It doesn't involve poverty.
The money is endless
The cars are superb
As they drive smoothly
Across the sunset.

For many they will never
Enter this opposite world,
As their situation is bringing them down.
All they can do, is stare and gaze,
Marked across, with
A big frown.

Sean Pursani
Deptford Green School, New Cross

London Town

Walkin' rand' London,
Seein' dem sytes.
Dat tawa ov London,
Dem Hawzis ov Parliament
All ov dem places make a wondaful tawn.

Seein' Buck 'awse,
Model ov Queen Vic,
All ov dem pubs,
Den 'alf make you proud to be British.

Brandon Hayward (13)
Deptford Green School, New Cross

The Trip

The luminous sky,
Flying high,
Above the sky,
Eating French fries.

Planes landing roughly,
Arriving safely,
Extremely drained,
It had rained.

On my way to my house,
Taking a shower,
Regaining my power.

In my bed,
Telling you what I read
Now it is night,
Turn off the light.

Huy Pham (13)
Deptford Green School, New Cross

The Road To Berlin

On my way to Berlin,
I saw the following . . .

An Ecuadorian who surprised,
A Costa Rican who couldn't win,
A Trinidadian who put up a fight,
A Swede and a Paraguayan who struggled.

Dutch and Portuguese men who fought,
An Argentine who embarrassed a Serbian, by six,
An Inorian who made their first appearance
And an Angolan who held a Mexican.

Iranian, Japanese, Koreans and Arabians,
Who didn't do Asia justice.

A Ghanaian who surprised the Czechs,
An American who could score one,
A Brazilian who didn't have the same spark,
A Croatian who was highly rated.

An Australian who just got through,
A Swiss that didn't let anything pass
A Tongan who rode a horse
A French man who head-butted an Italian.

An Italian who won it all.

And
An Englishman
Who let us all down - again!

Ashraf Muwawu (13)
Deptford Green School, New Cross

My Journey To School

My journey to school on Monday, was such a delight
It was warm and the sun was bright

My journey to school on Tuesday, was very funny
It was cold and not very sunny

My journey to school on Wednesday, was cold, but had a glow
It wasn't warm and there was no snow

My journey to school on Thursday, was sad
I nearly got detention, but I changed my ways and wasn't bad

My journey to school on Friday, was tiring
My brain was on full speed and the answers were firing.

Tia Elmi (12)
Deptford Green School, New Cross

Swimming

From downing in the pools
To holding my breath
And opening my eyes, going deeper in the waves.

Putting one arm forward,
Putting one arm back,
Putting one leg forward,
Just as fast as that.

One metre, two metres, three metres, four
I'm going through the water
Better than before.

From the future being dim
Me dream's now to swim
From the future being dimmer
I'm an Olympic swimmer.

William Angwa
Deptford Green School, New Cross

Sawf London Speak

You may think what we say,
Is kinda, sorta weird,
Or as we say down 'ere,
It's butters.

But you won',
Understand it,
It's Sawf London speak,
You see?

It's the accent from
Round 'ere kind,
Odd and strange,
Wowee!

Say what you like,
I speak like this!

David Palin
Deptford Green School, New Cross

An Old Stable Horse

One day, a stable horse dreamt to be wild and free,
Like the birds soaring through the sky.
He dreamt to have wisdom and knowledge,
Like the old dog who took care of him.
He dreamt to be tall and elegant,
Like a giraffe in the savannah.
He dreamt of being powerful and strong,
Like the stallion next door.
He dreamt of being fast and swift,
Like the grey train behind.
But now he was old and slow,
Like an old stable horse!

Mattias Evans (11)
Eltham College, Mottingham

Golden Eagle

I swam through the clouds,
Gliding through the soft moisture,
The animals on the ground,
Are ants to me.

I hatched from an egg, yesterday,
I rule the air, today,
I will die in the nest, tomorrow,
But I will still be the best at air.

I drift through the sky,
Looking, searching,
For my home in the mountains,
With my hatchlings waiting.

Finally, I saw it, my home,
Towered over me,
I soared to my nest,
To rest and to live another day.

Keerthikan Thirukkumar (12)
Eltham College, Mottingham

A Poem About A Tree

Tall and proud it stands
Touching the sky with its bony hands
Feeling the soil with its slender roots
With buds growing from its many shoots

Its leaves change throughout the year
A tall, imposing figure of fear
The branches sway in the cold night air
Leading a life without a care

The sound of a saw cuts through its bark
Leaving nothing but an empty mark
The once-tall tree falls through the air
The tall and proud, is now a chair.

Toby Fok (14)
Eltham College, Mottingham

Four Days Before 9/11

It was a lovely, fine day,
The seventh of September, was the date,
New York was where my dad was,
He isn't scared by Michael Jackson,
The scary man, whose case was being tried.

On the eighth day of the same month,
He enjoyed a meal, a starving man was he,
The friends that he met up with,
Oh, he had a great time,
On a beautiful night,
He called his wonderful wife.

On the ninth day in September,
Oh, what a day to remember!
Martin bought a new TV,
Which from a mile away, he could see,
He bought it for one thousand dollars,
A lot cheaper than in London.

On the tenth day of September,
He packed his belongings,
For tomorrow he leaves,
The lovely city he won't forget.

The eleventh day of September, 2001,
He left on a plane, only just before,
The terrorists gave a last visit,
To the Twin Towers, my dad just escaped!

James Riley (11)
Eltham College, Mottingham

Black Panther

Leaping from trees, he flies,
Pouncing to his prey's demise,
A shadow of the day
And night's forgotten friend, in a way.

Insatiable is its hunger,
Its voice growls as thunder,
That turns the strongest of men, to jellyfish,
Even if they see it or not.

Its claws are its scythes,
To grimly reap its prey,
Its eyes are two full moons,
But not to be seen as white, when it comes to noon.

Black is its name,
Black is its nature,
Black gets it through the night,
Black always seems to win the fight.

King of the night,
The sly, slaying jungle cat,
Never in or out of sight,
In the passing shadow, look out for the panther.

It is controlled by none
And seen by some,
The black panther is the night,
All that seek it, need to see the light.

Olu Arisekola (13)
Eltham College, Mottingham

The Murder Mystery

They should not have left him there alone,
Alone, except for the cat.
He was not old enough,
To be left alone in a basement flat,
Alone, except for the cat.
Was he dead?
Well, his parents are crying,
Yes, yes, he had been murdered,
Who was the murderer?
Where's the inspector when you need him?
You could still see the bullet hole entering the head.
He was bleeding, bleeding,
He was alone, except for the cat.
He was only two years old and worked on a field of animals,
Now he is dead and alone,
Alone, except for the cat.
His iPod was hanging out of his jacket,
His phone in his hand,
But where was his PSP?
Was it in his jacket?
Or was it behind him?

Lee Partridge (12)
Eltham College, Mottingham

My Generation

We live with lots of pressure
To keep us working hard,
To help us go to sleep at night
We buy the big, flash cars.

What isn't work, is play
But work takes all day
And when our day at school is finished,
We still have work to do,
Because don't forget the homework
And revision for tests too!

We may have lots of gadgets
To fill our lovely rooms,
PS3s, iPods and cell phones clutter up our desks.
We long to go out and play,
But Mum thinks she knows best.
She'll ferry us from A to B,
From tennis to piano,
But what we really want to do is play,
Have fun,
Be yourself!

Adam Broncz (12)
Eltham College, Mottingham

Lisa 581D

A new planet was born today,
Its name is Lisa 581D.
We crossed the vast ocean of space
And discovered it between waves of stars.

This planet is a frozen pot of gold,
Light years from any living organism,
In a minuscule solar system of its own,
This could be another Earth.

It could even replace Earth,
After all, it is floating in our galaxy,
But can it fulfil the requirements of people lost from a planet
Burnt out by global warming?

James Morrison (12)
Eltham College, Mottingham

My Generation

A big TV screen,
Will make today's children gleam,
Burgers and fries,
Makes them mesmerised.

A room looking neat,
Makes their hearts miss a beat,
Natural daylight,
Is a fright.

A chocolate packet,
Will make the children go manic,
The only exercise they get,
Is surfing the net.

A PlayStation is what makes
My generation!

William Epps (11)
Eltham College, Mottingham

My Generation

M y generation is always told, 'Our generation was the best!'
Y et we're kids, still to accomplish

G lobal warming staring us in the face
E nergy wasted every day by us and our parents
N ot a pretty life ahead for us, is it
E co-friendly cars roaming our roads
R obots all over the shop
A t least we can use computers for our coursework
T Vs in cars
I nternet in every room
O nly we can live up to the challenges we are faced with
N o one else, just us.

Charlie Murphy (12)
Eltham College, Mottingham

Ode To A Coke Can

Oh, wondrous Coke can,
Your roundness is divine.
I can see my reflection on your phosphorescent body,
You make me effervescent.
You are my Corona,
When I pull your flap,
Your fizzle indulges me with glee.
I smell your heavenly odour
And drink your delicious liquid,
I feel as if I have fallen from Heaven.
You are with me everywhere I go,
Through rain and snow
And in an exam, you get me going.
You dazzle my eyes, which become paralysed,
I read the *'Best Served Chilled'* label.
Oh, wondrous and cold Coke can,
We shall never be parted,
For you are my master!

Robbie Campbell (13)
Eltham College, Mottingham

The Internet

An invisible shield around the world
An entangled net, no spider dare compete
Does it exist? Does it not?
Where does it live?
Hardware?
Software?
Questions I cannot answer
Always there but never seen, a living organism.

Opening wireless network
Information transfer
Round the world it goes
In a flash, it's there
Ideas
Facts
News
Messages
Gossip
Mind out!
There's an email coming, a big, fat, mean one
Look at all those viruses
I wonder what they're thinking?
What's that?
A firewall
Oh, good, I'm through
What's this?
Wickipedia, I see
Stuffed full of knowledge, ideas, pictures
What do you want to know?
All the world, at your fingertips
Just a few keys away.

William Jessop (12)
Eltham College, Mottingham

My Generation

My generation is the techno-generation;
On the computer before breakfast
Text your friend before school
Driven to school in a 'Chelsea tractor'
DS's all round at break time!
PCs in every classroom
That's my generation.

Turkey Twizzlers for lunch
No 'Jamie's' meals in this school!
Kids too fat to play football,
That's only for the TV,
'Research' on the Internet for coursework,
Reading reference books isn't for us!
That's my generation.

Down to the newsagent at the end of school,
Stuff their faces with Doritos and chocolate,
Back home in the 'tractor',
For PS3, Xbox and more!
That's my generation.

Lazing like slugs on their DFS couch,
Watching a DVD on their HD-TV,
Their only exercise - for their jaws and thumbs,
'Chatting' with their friends on MSN,
Solitary in their bedroom.
No reading before sleep,
Just turn off the PC at five past three.
That's my generation.

Laurence Hill (12)
Eltham College, Mottingham

So Much To Do, Yet So Little Time

So close to death, yet so little time,
How shall I spend these moments of mine?
Should I forgive or should I remind?
So much to do, yet so little time.

I ask many questions, yet no one replies,
I am all alone in this room, where I'll die,
Is this where it ends? Is this where I die?
In this plain white room, where the sun does not shine.

When the time comes, when I do die,
I want to be out, below that blue sky,
I want to be free; back in that fresh air,
So, that's where I go, my mind takes me there.

I shut my eyes tight; I feel the light breeze,
The sun on my face, the buzz of the bees,
The luscious green grass, the clear, bright blue sky,
My family's there and I wave goodbye.

Michael Jacobs (13)
Eltham College, Mottingham

My Generation

My generation,
Living in a world of globalisation,
We can now fly rockets into space,
Or provide someone with a new face!
However, poverty still rages throughout the world
And in Iraq, bombs are hurled,
We can travel around at thousands of miles per hour
And fuel our homes on nuclear power,
Technology is part of all our lives
And teens roam the streets, feeling the need for knives,
Drink and drugs are a serious topic,
But we can develop robots that are microscopic,
Just as any, we have our faults:
Genocide, war, terrorism, assaults,
But we've certainly made the world something new
And I'm sure we'll continue to.

Josh Carty (14)
Eltham College, Mottingham

The Stalker

It is on the stalk again
Following a majestic creature
With a pelt of burning orange and black
He raises his head, smelling prey
Pounding after the prey
Crack!
The burning orange and black pelt falls
Just a small hole to show what happened
The prey races away but the stalker
Sees the majestic orange and black
And drags the fallen creature back to its lair

It is on the stalk again
Following the king of the jungle
With a shaggy mane
He walks back to his pride
The stalker bides his time, the rest of the pride go hunting
Crack!
The shaggy mane falls
Just a small hole to show what happened
The others come rushing back but to no avail
The stalker shoos them off
And drags the fallen creature back to its lair

The burning orange and black
Meets the shaggy mane
Distant cousins but with no life
They have been killed by the deadliest creature
The human and his gun.

Adam Knox (13)
Eltham College, Mottingham

Chicken Farm Poem

Walk around
Peck at food squashed into a box, others
Like me have no idea what's outside
I'm stuck here, confined to a tiny grain of sand
Unable to escape
Others push me when the men come
They grab us and cut our throats
Like we were nothing more than a profession
To them.

Millions of us in one room, no light
No grass underfoot, just darkness
Disease and deathly infections all around
Boxed in, squashed with others, no freedom.

I'm young and small
They want to feed me so I'm big
Fat, like the ones he drags away every day
And I'm big now, much like the other ones they use
I push to the back, hoping he won't see the fattest one
At the back, he spots me
I flutter in panic and I am dragged away . . .

His machines scrape me as
Moving along a conveyor belt, I feel sleepy
The satanic, metal machines
Push me, pluck at my feathers
My foot is green and sore from infection
Then a knife runs
Across my neck, smooth and cold, it cuts me open
A few last flutters of panic and then . . . nothing.

Chris Kruger (13)
Eltham College, Mottingham

The Winter Woods

I gaze at my reflection on the icy lake
I leave great big footprints as I trample through the snow
I hear the frosty wind's breezy whisper;
I hear the howl of the winter wolves.

The beam of moonlight shines through the wood
Guiding my footsteps as I walk
The crunch of snow is music to my ears
But the chilling silence threatens.

The trees are standing naked and bare
The night is as cold as the snow
I can feel the snowflakes melt on my head
I can feel the deathly stillness.

The cold sends frost shivers down my spine
The occasional rustle in the snow-scattered bushes
The creatures watch me as I leave the winter woods
And slowly
Slip
Away . . .

Alex Robinson (12)
Eltham College, Mottingham

The Deep, Dark Cave

I am sitting in my cave and the dark is closing in
Light may still come shining
But the dark is closing in
I sit and stare and listen to the silence
I hear my heart beating like a giant drum inside my body
I stand up and all the light is gone, but one dot
Then Death appears and I am scared
It reaches out but I escape, out of reach
And run towards the spec of light
But I am just too late, Death has caught me
I am gone.

Bertie Rowbotham (13)
Eltham College, Mottingham

My Generation

In an age of technology,
Where everyone expects an apology,
In a multicultural society,
We've got to fly the flag of diversity,
In a time of teenage murder
And drugs being a real earner,
My generation need the education to resist temptation,
With medical improvements,
We'll be here to make several movements,
One thing's for sure,
My generation,
Is going to be a sensation!

Rory O'Connor Massingham (13)
Eltham College, Mottingham

My Generation

A large crowd
Staring at the body of a dying teen
This is becoming a daily occurrence
Since street knives came into being.

Stabbed, bleeding, lying on the floor
Ambulance sirens wailing
On their way
But probably too late.

Parents coming
Stinking of fear
Ambulance arrives
Check the pulse

Death fills the air.

Jamie Phillips (13)
Eltham College, Mottingham

Think Before You Drink

I gaze upon the shimmering star,
With a heavy heart going to the bar,
Making my problems seem afar,
It just sounds quite bizarre.

It makes a man full of deep lust,
With it you truly must not trust,
It makes you crazy because it's not just,
Don't go too far, that's a must.

I cross the bar with my first tread,
I thought of one thing in my head,
'Don't drink too much,' a voice said,
I was thirsty and did not think ahead.

I could not stop, I was hypnotised,
But I kept on drinking, paralysed,
I was scared and had not realised,
It was too late, time for my demise.

Falling slowly to the ground,
In the alley, I was found,
Unable to move, not making a sound,
A pool of blood emerging around.

I thought to myself, *was I dead?*
Before I knew it, I was in a hospital bed,
I should have listened to my head,
But now, I'm fighting for my life instead.

Zohaib Siddiqui (14)
Eltham College, Mottingham

Plight Of The Child Soldier

They run from bush to bush, as gunfire crackles overhead,
Children's bodies lay on the ground, motionless,
Trampled underfoot.
The other soldiers in their Mickey Mouse T-shirts scurried forward,
They held their rocks up high in defiance, ready to kill the enemy.
Some scooped up the dropped guns,
It seemed like fun at first,
But
All knew what really waited,
Death.
Three months ago, a helicopter flew into the village,
Men came running out,
Crouching down, aiming, shooting,
Bullets rattled off the helicopter,
The men took the children away.
The village was filled with the grief of mothers.
The new recruits were taught how to shoot,
How to kill with stones, knives,
They were bundled into a truck,
Which would take them to the government base.
These children had no experience of war,
Some cried,
Some screamed,
Some shouted for their mothers,
Some did not care, they were orphans.
The truck stopped and they clambered out,
They ran from bush to bush, as gunfire crackled overhead,
As so many had done before.

James Prior (14)
Eltham College, Mottingham

The Ballad Of Baron Bellvadire

Hundreds of years ago
In those days of yore
There were men who could forgo
Life's fineries like velvet, azure.

Our Baron Bellvadire
Was not one of those men.
He held his luxuries dear
Leaving unpleasantness to other men.

He built up his Bellvadire Hall
With soldiers and retainers
So his star would never fall
Yet his gluttony left his granaries with no remainders.

He raised massive tithes
To afford his massive gait.
His peasants sharpened their knives
To hang the taxman from his gate.

The Baron boiled
Let loose his dogs
His extravagance foiled
His table empty of hogs.

The soldiers murdered
The serfs rebelled
For the wretch they murdered
Bodies like trees were felled.

The day was ended
The Baron won
The peasant dead pretended
The rich then had their fun.

Once night had fallen
And the Baron gone a'bed
The peasants rose when fallen
They were no longer dead

For the peasants had hid
From the Baron's horde
Now when their leaders bid
They slaughtered the courtiers bored.

They burst into the Baron's Hall
Beheading all they found
They burnt it so it would fall
Into an ashen mound.

The Baron screamed
Like a child, he whimpered
As the fire before him gleamed
And the floor below him splintered.

David Long (13)
Eltham College, Mottingham

The Day London Was Afraid

The claustrophobic cabin
The distant beat blaring from the man's headphones
The engaged look of the woman reading
The focused eyes, transfixed on the chewing gum
Decorated floor
The hissing of the doors opening
The exit of people travelled
The entrance of people travelling
The increased intensity in the focused eyes
The push of a button
The blast
The darkness and the shock
The blood and the screaming
The loss of lives
The tears of the survivors
The silence of the dead
The fear-stricken London.

Thomas Lavin (14)
Eltham College, Mottingham

My Generation

The doors of the bus swing open,
Number nine,
I swipe my card through the scanner,
The aroma of Burger King assaults my nostrils,
A group of hooded adolescents play their intolerably loud music
From the back of the bus,
An elderly woman follows me on, carrying her Waitrose bag,
I wonder if she is carrying a bomb as well.

Suspicious looks as I take my seat next to a plump,
Double-chinned city worker,
Dressed in some designer pinstripe suit,
The gum on the floor sticks to the soles of my trainers,
Sweat trickles down the back of my parka
As I draw closer and closer to my departure from this world,
I think back to my homeland and I'm tortured,
By the memory of the slaughter of my friends and family,
Butchered carcasses,
I remember why I am here.

We stop again.

I reach into my shirt and push the detonator.

Alex Jones (14)
Eltham College, Mottingham

The Ghost Train

The train was full with bustling people, all heading off to work.
He got on by himself;
Everyone glanced at him, but gave no second thought.

Loudly did everybody talk, but I wonder, did they realise,
Only not the lonely man.
Now and then, he looked at his watch; he seemed to have a plan
Down the track the train went, swallowed up into eight minutes
                                        of merciful darkness:
On the dot of 8.50am, a noise ripped through London.
Never was the lonely man seen again - in carriage three

Bodies flew and people died screaming.
Overhead, shrapnel shot and on the floor, blood lay streaming;
Men and women crumpled in the blast as the train staggered
                                        over like a dying lamb -
Blood gushing from his side.
I the carriage, bodies lay ripped and broken,
Nver to be woken,
Gone forever,
Strewn in the wake of the ghost train.

Stephen Hall (13)
Eltham College, Mottingham

My Life

In front of the TV we sit
And on the PS3 we play
Colours bright
We dim the light
With our eyes glued to the screen

My imp, we watch; it bounds around
My friends stare in horror
As it bounds
It starts to chant
'I love the mansion we're in!'

Outside the shop the football flies
Then loud noise erupts around
My phone is ringing!
I close the text
And down the road I sprint

Now we're at school
We want to play ball
But the teachers never let us!

Nathan Stables (11)
Eltham College, Mottingham

Career Opportunity - Wacky TV Cat

Are you crazy, stupid and
An idiot?
Do you enjoy dying
Then being chopped up?

Your duties will include being
Blown up, shot and
Squashed

Preference will be given
To those candidates
Who come equipped with
Their own coffin and funeral money

NB mice management accepts
No responsibility for
Loss of life before show.

Colby John Dann (12)
Eltham College, Mottingham

How Was Your Day At The Office, Dear?

How was your day at the office, dear?

The usual stuff
I fought with a knight upon a horse
Joined the army, a special force
I went on a ride to the moon and back
Rode upon a dragon's back
Took a trip to the country Gaul
Stayed awhile and saw the Roman Empire fall
Took a swim with some whales
Went to the future, England fails
Went to war
Couldn't believe some of the things I saw
I was knighted by many queens
Arrested some of the most dangerous fiends
I learnt a couple of foreign languages
Got blown up, the doctors covered me in bandages
Saved the future president's life
Went back to the future, it ends in strife
Got caught in a nuclear missile attack
And then decided it was time to come back.

That's lovely dear, your dinner's ready!

Cameron Lester (12)
Eltham College, Mottingham

In The Limelight

Everyone around me is clapping,
The spotlight I cannot help trapping,
The lights all around are shining,
The public, celebrity miming.

The others like me are coping,
But I am just hoping,
That I can see the night out,
I wish that he'd turn that light out!

As I walk through the door,
Making sure I'm avoiding the floor,
I find myself in a massive hall,
Big enough for a royal ball!

I go through another door,
The size of which I have not seen before,
The lights are back,
The room is red, the seats are black.

I move through to my seat,
No longer feeling like fresh meat,
The awards are about to begin,
The crowds are making a din!

Jonathan Hiscock (14)
Eltham College, Mottingham

Homeless Man

He sits, cocooned in a pile of filthy blankets and newspapers,
Dejected and rejected, his hopes quashed by poverty and loneliness,
His few possessions stashed in ancient plastic bags,
Tied together with string,
A sorrowful sight by the side of the road.

His face is sunken, his skin sallow, cracked with age
And coated in grime,
His grey, unkempt beard, matted with yesterday's meagre meal,
His long coat hunched over his shoulders,
Reaching down to his old split shoes,
Only his eyes show a glimmer of hope,
Like a doorway to another reality.

A scruffy terrier, his constant companion, lies bored beside him,
A flea-ridden tail between two gaunt legs,
Large, baleful eyes survey the street,
He sniffs occasionally at a small, empty bowl,
His dark, mottled frame barely distinguishable
From the surrounding debris.

Commuters emerge from the nearby train station,
Most avert their eyes,
He looks, a practised pleading, at the well-dressed
Lawyers and bankers returning home,
A few drop coins into his polystyrene cup,
Then scurry on, unspeaking,
He counts the coins and drinks the last few drops
Of cider from a can.

I see him every day, but our lives never intersect,
After all, there's nothing I can do, he's made his choice, hasn't he?
We drive on past, his life just a moment of discomfort in our busy day,
I'll never finish up like that
Will I?

Hamish Hamilton (13)
Eltham College, Mottingham

Late For Registration

'Sorry I'm late, Sir!'
Probably the most commonly said phrase
Within English speaking secondary schools.
How can this be? If . . .
We have bells which ring in advance,
There are such things as watches and phones,
Which have the time on them,
Maybe a surprise to you schoolboys,
But apparently we're meant to be eager to learn.

How is it possible then,
To be late, day in, day out?

Observe:
Through countless theories and formulas
And first-hand experience of being late most days,
I have come to the following conclusion:
Teenagers are lazy, unless the matter is for their own,
Short-term benefit,
Fact!

Solutions come and go,
With no real effect.

Observe:
Through countless theories and formulas
And first-hand experience of being late most days,
I have come to the following conclusion:
Teenagers need an incentive to be on time for something
If it is within their personal concern,
Fact!

School councils are formed
And ideas are bounced,
But none come of anything.

The answer?
Look the teenager in the eye, show him a detention slip
And tell him to get inside . . .
And then add . . .
'Or else!'

Thomas Michael Ian Wilson (14)
Eltham College, Mottingham

Jaguar

He waits,
He waits until the cover of darkness,
Which will conceal him,
Darkness comes,
When it comes, he moves,
Sneaking silently down the slender tree trunk,
His long claws gripping it, like a vice.

He hears a sound,
He stops, suspended in time,
Not even breathing, not responding
To the blood being sucked out of him by blood-sucking fleas,
He waits, he waits until he is sure the enemy has gone,
Then he sees what he has searched for,
A deer,
He pounces, flying through the air as gracefully as a ballet dancer,
The deer standing still, stupefied.

Its life completely drained out of it,
In a nanosecond,
The unfortunate creature was still,
Its frail body limp, lost.

The jaguar sits, satisfied,
Surrounded by forest,
Where life seems to have stopped, insane,
Transfixed by this wonder of the world.

Matthew Burgess (13)
Eltham College, Mottingham

The Seasons

Summer is people melting in the boiling sun,
The burning sun shines bright across the land.
Happy children playing and having fun,
Whilst stuck inside an airport,
While holiday plans are done.

Autumn is the season for leaf fights,
Strong winds blowing kites.
With animals scurrying around, searching for food,
Loads of trees without their leaves,
So there are barely any lights.

Winter consists of smooth snow, glistening in the sparkling sky,
No birds in England want to fly.
The icy winds sway through the silver trees,
Snowflakes dance to the frosty ground,
This is the season for hibernation.

Spring is a magical time of year,
The bare trees suddenly appear,
Pink and white as blossom comes,
Dew green grass sways side to side,
As winter is left behind.

Harrison Wilson (12)
Eltham College, Mottingham

Through My Shell-Like

Lift lightly to your ear,
A small, smooth, colourful
And spiral shell,
Off the sieved sandy beach, we all love.
The sea waves are magic,
As the sea's spirits whisper in your ear,
Shh, shh, shh, shh, shh . . .
Telling you to
Surf through the dense,
Sandy, salt, spectacular waves of the web,
Into the land of
Marine, colourful sea monsters,
You scuba dive
And walk on the big bed of the ocean floor,
Between the spiky, living, moving coral,
Magical seashells of the soundly sleeping silent,
Water
Mini-beasts await,
They move,
Slow as turtles,
Along the bed of weeds and colourful coral.
I step, wondering and thinking,
Away from the Web
Far from my keyboard,
Near to home are
My hundreds of friends,
My brother and two sisters.
I am a brave man,
I am an only nerd in my family and form,
I must change,
I guess I am lucky to still have friends,
Nerds are not a good sign in my generation,
I must change
I must change . . .

Aman Gupta (11)
Eltham College, Mottingham

The Vase And The Shotgun

Click-click, chick-chick,
The gun was loaded,
The hammer was back
And the handle eroded.

The trigger was pulled,
A split second of silence,
Both barrels blazing,
With vigour and violence.

The vase was hit,
The sharp shards scattered,
The wall was in pieces
And the carpet now tattered.

The firearm was lowered,
With debris on the floor,
It was the end
And the vase was no more.

Sebastian Wiseman (13)
Eltham College, Mottingham

My Nightmare In The Class

Another day, another nightmare
From the children in the class
They are as noisy as hyenas
And monkeys jumping up and down
When would this nightmare ever end?
I just wish this day would end!

The days are hard and most things are easy
And the children are like a swarm of bees coming to me
And I work all day, it's like saying, 'Hey!' Again and again
When would this nightmare end?
I just wish this day would end!

Tomer Banai (12)
JFS School, Harrow

My School Day

Another day begun, as it's 7.01
You're still not awake and your marking's not done
Your shower isn't refreshing, your eggs aren't runny
It's really not that funny.

You trip on your way to school, you fall in the hall,
The toilets overflow in the bathroom stall
The gym door is locked for the basketball game
The headteacher greets you by a different name.

Your class is as wild as an elephant without a peanut
All the girls scream, punch and head butt
I wish that they were as sweet as the cherry on your cupcake
And that my headteacher said, 'This school is closed, mate.'

Your class is the poisoned apple in Snow White
If your child got an F, it's considered as bright
Your classroom is hot, the pupils see your sweaty pits
Your board pens go missing, you throw big fits.

The lunches are lumpy and taste of blue cheese
Most of the children are off with something called fleas
You take extra classes as the sub didn't arrive
I guess you could say, at least she will stay alive.

Unlucky me, you can clearly see my stress marks
The children all sound like a dog when it barks
Then it makes you wonder why you woke up this morning
This job makes my life even more boring.

Emily Curtis (11)
JFS School, Harrow

The Holocaust

I'm an evacuee,
Why can't those Nazis let us be?
I've only got my teddy bear
Doesn't Hitler even care?

I took some pens and a book,
Mums are crying, I can't look.
I'll miss my very best friends,
Why does friendship have to end?

I packed my bags in the night,
Cold and confused, I shivered with fright.
Why do I have to leave my home?
Why do I have to leave all alone?

Look at me, look at you,
You are German, I'm a Jew.
How come you're allowed to be free?
It really isn't fair for me.

The Nazis with snarling breath,
Walking beside them, is the figure of Death.
Will we go, left or right?
Need some peace, need some light.

We're going to kill Hitler,
Stab him to his death.
We hope to be there,
When he takes his final breath.

Asal Reyhanian (11)
JFS School, Harrow

The Devils!

It all started when I woke up this morning
Got up, got dressed, got to school
Bang! It was the devils' tricks
They call it ball on car
I call it detention!

Next, they stuck glue to my chair
I screamed at them
That gave them a scare
For some reason they apologised
This was very rare.

. . . Next lesson was science
We made stink bombs
Yes, it was silly, stupid, so frustrating
By now I should be fainting!

You not bored yet?
Guess what? The devils bought a pet!
It was a dog, but I thought it was a frog
To top it off, they hit me with a big, fat log!

Last lesson, anxious for the bell
What's that I smell?
It's freedom round the corner
Ten, nine, eight, seven, six . . .
Oh no, I fell
Five, four, three, two, one
Hooray! Saved by the bell!

Michael Simons (12)
JFS School, Harrow

Why Am I A Teacher?

My hard day starts
At about eight in the morning.
By the time I'm at school,
I'm always still yawning.

The children are so loud,
As loud as a drum.
Maybe they are in maths,
I could give them a maths sum.

They start to come into class
And get their books out.
But there is always someone forgetful,
I know that, without a doubt.

I take their progress record
And give them a bad note.
Some of them make noises,
Like a cow or a goat.

Break is the best part,
The best part of the day.
At least for the children it is,
They can scream and play.

Whenever I come to school,
I am always so tired.
But I have to keep my head up,
Otherwise I'll get fired.

The children are a spark,
A spark of my day.
If only they were quiet,
Quiet in any way.

Kelli Wegoda (11)
JFS School, Harrow

No Way, It's School Again!

No! It can't be! There will be no school for me
Why do I have to wake up so early, just to teach boring PE?

Have my breakfast, fruit, tea, bread,
But I really want to go back to bed!

On my way to school again,
It's a miniature version of Hell,
Just hoping they don't chime that bell.

Finally, what seemed a year to wait,
Time to face my dreadful fate.

The boys and girls come inside,
They're like a thorn in my backside.

Sleeping sloths come out of class,
Looking like they're in a trance.

Can't inspire this lazy lot,
Forgive them, I think not!

Lunchtime, maybe I can get a rest,
Oh no! Here comes that dreadful pest!

'Beating up another kid,' I say
And all he did was walk away.

Back to lessons, teaching maths,
Learning how to deal with money,
For once, this class was as sweet as honey.

Last lesson of the day,
Now I will make them pay.

Sending children to detention,
Serves them right for not paying attention.

Back in the comfort of my home,
Feet up, watching a series about Rome.

Not quite over yet,
Thinking about reports and sets.

Weekend, set the clock for ten,
Beep! Beep! Oh no, it's school again!

Andrew Roth (11)
JFS School, Harrow

A Nightmare Come Alive

The pupils are a herd of elephants
Thudding round my head,
It's like a nightmare come alive
While I'm in my bed.

I'm in school,
I have to act cool
And calm,
But really, it's like a crowd of bees
Swarming round my arm,
A nightmare come alive!

The pupils are noisy and playful
And some are rude,
Which puts me in a real bad mood!
I need a rest,
I don't feel my best,
A nightmare come alive!

Papers and pens,
As annoying as hens,
Clucking and chucking away,
It's like the pens on paper
Being used all day,
A nightmare come alive!

But, other than that,
School is great,
I can't wait to go in
And teach Year Eight,
A dream of fluffy clouds.

Sophie Corper (11)
JFS School, Harrow

Revenge Of The Children

Being a teacher in this school,
Is like losing a game of pool.
The pupils are like monkeys in school
And they would probably rather go to shul.

Being in school is like being in a cell,
With a very annoying ringing bell.
The pupils have smiles like snakes,
When they are up to no good.
They are afraid to tell me,
But they know they should.

The pupils are like a group of mice,
Making annoying noises once or twice.
When you tell them to be quiet, they don't listen,
Maybe we need to change their seating position.

I really dislike school,
Because the children think they rule.
I dread marking a particular student's test,
Because they think they are the best.
The pupils think they're pretty perfectly good students!

Jonathan Richards (12)
JFS School, Harrow

My Struggle With Children

My head is hurting, my throat is sore,
I can't bare these children anymore!
I teach all day, at a humungous school,
I don't know why I do it, I feel such a fool!
The laughter in the playground,
The crying of a cut,
The shouting of the arguments,
Leading to doors slamming shut.
It sounds like a jungle,
All the children going wild,
I wouldn't want any of them
To be my child.
Maths, English, science and art,
Whatever subject I'm teaching, they never take part.
The children are as sly as cats,
Some of them are as dirty as rats!
The school is like a prison cell,
I wait anxiously for the end of the day bell.
My head is hurting, my throat is sore,
I can't bare these children anymore!

Charlotte Kaye (11)
JFS School, Harrow

A Weary Day At School

My days are long
And most things go wrong.
I work all the time, which makes me tired,
Sometimes I wish that for this job, I was not hired!
> I wish I didn't have to go to school
> Being a teacher makes me look like a fool!

My pupils are as loud as drums,
What can I do? I have to take whatever comes.
Some are clever parrots, but most are lazy sheep,
Sometimes at night, I get hardly any sleep.
> I wish I didn't have to go to school
> Being a teacher makes me look like a fool!

In the mornings, I dread to go to school,
Knowing that I'll have all those papers on my desk,
I think that my job is just too cruel!
Waiting and waiting, but the bell just won't ring,
Oh, how I wish my job was more bling!
> I wish I didn't have to go to school
> Being a teacher makes me look like a fool!

Writing reports is the best,
It's the only time pupils suck up to me
And do well in their tests!
It's not that bad, after all,
It's just a long, tiring day, at school.

Fiona Bleetman (12)
JFS School, Harrow

To Be On The Stage

To perform on the stage,
To act my heart out,
To go through the script, page after page,
Oh, I wish I could be on the stage!

To have fame and glory,
To have fans who love me,
To act out a story,
Oh, I wish I could be on the stage!

Each day thinking the same thing,
Dreaming a dream,
Wishing a wish,
Oh, I wish I could be on the stage!

Projecting my voice,
Moving my body,
Bowing to the audience,
Oh, I wish I could be on the stage!

But it's only a dream,
A silly, little dream,
One of many others,
Oh, I wish I could be on the stage!

Fading away?
Not my thing,
I love to dance, act and sing!
Oh, I wish I could be on the stage!

Daniella Myers (11)
JFS School, Harrow

Could My Day Get Better?

The first day of school
Can be so cruel,
I got inside my car,
The car broke down
With a very loud bang.
Could my day get better?

I came into the school, which was so massive in my sight,
Kids were running while the teachers were so cunning,
I felt like I was in the zoo,
Not knowing what to do,
Some pupils came up to me, welcoming me.
Could my day get better?

I think I found my class,
But unfortunately there was no one to ask,
So I came in with a smile,
My eyes were gleaming to know,
Is this the place for me or should I go?
Could my day get better?

Ok, to be new can be harsh,
The pupils are like a new generation, a new piece of art,
The cafeteria is refreshing,
The lunch ladies are as clean as water drops,
Swerving each dish, waiting to stop.
Could my day get better?

Now my poem is done,
I hope it was fun,
Knowing how new teachers feel
And next time you see a teacher, make a deal,
That when she is new and wants to work,
Don't make it harsh, make it work!

Ariella Kramer (11)
JFS School, Harrow

The Cheeky Children

The children always
Come out to play
Why can't they be like horses
Who just eat hay?

Sometimes they're noisy
And sometimes they're rude
Sometimes I feel like
Stuffing them down a toilet tube!

The pupils are like
Barbarians in a class
If it was a game show
I would just say, 'Pass!'

Every lesson
They make a *bash* or *bosh*
With about two minutes to go
That's when they still on their tosh!

The pupils are a crowd of frogs
Jumping in and out of your life
Thank goodness they don't get carried away
And pull out a knife!

And now it's time
To end the poem
And if you don't know my name
It's Mr Cohen!

So, thank you for reading
I appreciate it a lot
Because I really want the children
To go back into their cots!

Josh Gurvitz (11)
JFS School, Harrow

The Pupils' Classroom

I wake up today
Dreading my day
Knowing that I have school today
Kids screaming
Throwing around
Bullies picking on kids which makes people shout
Every day
Always the same pupils
Are as horrible as a bundle of monkeys
That make people play with clay
French, well, where do we start?
The more they learn, the more they laugh
Science, oh no, kids mixing chemicals about
All the time *bash! Ba-bang!*
English, well, don't say that again
Or you will be thrown out with a great, big
Bang!

Georgia Mooney (12)
JFS School, Harrow

The Fridge

Oh, how happy I would be,
If only I could see,
A fridge in my room,
While I'm watching TV.

The fridge would be blue,
My walls also, too,
The room is so cool,
Like a big swimming pool.

Inside the fridge, it's cold,
But that's not how it was sold,
When the fridge gets old,
Inside there may be mould!

Katie Barker (12)
JFS School, Harrow

Teacherphobia

Teaching is very hard work,
Pupils can get distracted by words,
It is annoying, there and then,
But some of my students,
Don't even have a pen!

Some of them rap, here and there,
Others sing, like growling bears.

And at the end of the day,
I have a huge headache,
But I feel an accomplishment,
That I have helped the children,
Get a better future,
They think that I am boring,
But what they don't know,
Is that I am a famous beat boxer!

Jack Shlomi (12)
JFS School, Harrow

About Me

There was a boy with curly hair
Who lived in a huge bear
His dream was footie
His young star was Sooty
That boy with curly hair
With his wiggly, wormy hair
He got noticed a lot
As sneaky as a snake
Thought his hair was fake
He had a friend called Alice
Who wanted to live in a palace
She liked it a lot
And ate out of a pot
His great friend, Alice.

Joseph Eskenazy (12)
JFS School, Harrow

Nature Is Beauty

The crashing waves on the sunset sea,
The shimmering dolphins splashing free,
Eroded rocks make an exotic view,
A stunning archway to look straight through.

The wailing waterfall makes its way,
Down the soft and sandy bay,
The palm trees swiftly sway in the breeze,
Shadowy figures revolve from the trees.

The horizon lights like a ball of fire,
A photograph image, enough to inspire,
The screeching seagulls swoop the air,
They spread their wings without a care.

Silhouette figures on the evening cruise,
The moon comes out and the colours suffuse,
As darkness falls and the stars reflect,
The rippling sea is just perfect.

When dusk fell upon the silvery sea,
Night began and the waves were free,
Eroded rocks, as dark as coal,
The day has ended within your soul.

Sarah Shamia (12)
JFS School, Harrow

Plans For Tomorrow

I'm sitting here, at my desk
Trying to concentrate
It's nearly midnight
It's really late

I'm marking the tests
They did in class
Hoping each one of them
Is going to pass

Thinking about
What to teach tomorrow
Telling them
What books they should borrow

Sometimes in the hallway
Like lions, they roar
But I have to make sure
In class, they don't snore

My job is teaching
It has to be done
Sometimes it's hard
But mostly, it's fun.

David Schmidt (11)
JFS School, Harrow

Untitled

There was a boy called Mark,
Who loved going to the park,
He rode on his skates,
With a few mates,
Then got scared by a dog's bark.

He got pulled to the ground,
By the small hound,
There were scratches and licks,
Some punches and kicks,
He got beaten by the speed of sound.

It started to get dark,
In the giant park,
He ran off home,
All the way to Rome,
Oh, that boy called Mark.

Idan Levy (12)
JFS School, Harrow

I Knew That I Could

I am trying to think of a poem,
But I don't know what to do.
I know I will finally show them,
That there are lots of things to do.

It is really, really hard,
I am getting a little stuck.
I'd rather make a card,
But I guess I don't have any luck.

I've finally written my poem,
I think it is very good.
I knew that I would show them,
I knew that I could.

James Crown (12)
JFS School, Harrow

There Is An Animal I Know

There is an animal I know,
That likes to be in the snow,
He has got a big, furry coat
And he often sleeps on a boat.

There is an animal I know,
That has no toes,
It slithers all day and slithers all night
And he likes to fight.

There is an animal I know,
That is not fast, not slow,
He has big ears,
But he has no fears.

Sharon Bamberg (12)
JFS School, Harrow

The Chocolate

It was white and creamy
It made me dreamy
Chocolate, chocolate.

With a side of milk
As smooth as silk
Chocolate, chocolate.

Try and take it away from me
Regret it, you will see
Chocolate, chocolate.

It can make your teeth rot
It melts if it's hot
Chocolate, chocolate.

I'm a chocoholic
Watch me jump and frolic!

Kelly Levy (12)
JFS School, Harrow

The Nightmare Come True

The kids are as wild as hyenas,
About to chase you till you stop.

As soon as you fall into their hands,
There's no way out for freedom,
You tell them to be quiet, but they don't listen,
In the end, they get tired, so they're not so loud,
Then the headmaster comes in and they all do you proud.

When you have a headache and you feel like leaving,
But you know you can't, because you'll upset the kids,
Although they are annoying and noisy,
At the end of the day they leave, gleaming.

They leave the classroom in a big mess
And you want to leave it, because you are all stressed,
You get all angry and hit the pencil pot,
Then you leave and go to the parking lot.

You get in your car and drive home,
Having to mark the work that they did during the day,
You go out to the park whilst walking your dog,
It's raining and you can't wait till it goes away,
Then you go home and watch TV,
Whilst drinking a hot cup of tea.

Late at night, you go to bed,
To get rid of your headache and rest your head,
You hope tomorrow never comes,
So you don't have to teach.

Nicholas Bloch (12)
JFS School, Harrow

The Perfect Pet

I said to my mum, I would like the perfect pet
So, on a day, we went to find the perfect vet
There were so many to choose from, I could not decided
So we started with the cats, who were one-eyed.

There were ones big and small, thin and fat
But I did not want a cat, so that was that
Because I wanted the perfect pet
But we still have not seen that one yet

We walked over to the dogs
They were playing with toy frogs
There was one with fur as white as snow
But that one had been taken long ago

I wanted to get the perfect pet
The perfect one that was in this vet
There were snakes slithering all around
But they were not making a sound

I would quite like a fluffy rabbit
But then I will have to get into the habit
Of cleaning its den every night
Well, I thought to myself, *that could be all right!*

And now I've found the perfect pet
But which colour should I get
In the corner there lay a rabbit that was red
And so I said
I would like that rabbit and take it home from this vet.

Ella Bernie (11)
JFS School, Harrow

Why Do I Have To Come Here Every Day?

Why do I have to come here every day?
Is it because I like to teach?
No way!
I'd rather be at home,
With my son, Salomé.
I almost forget my lovely boy,
Especially how much he's such a joy!

My pupils are not nice to each other,
Not since the last time, I remember!
They are always very loud
And they seem quite proud.
But if only the headmaster would see
And maybe feel sorry for me!

My husband is very lazy,
My mum can't help (she's going crazy!)
My dad is unfortunately up there,
So all he can do is stare
At how his daughter is not coping
And wishing for success, oh, how I'm hoping!

I have never had free time,
I've never had a chance to let my anger out
And do a crime!
Only because the pupils are always on my back
And never giving me time to relax.
But not everyone's bad though,
Not everyone hits you with big piles of snow.

Why do I have to come here every day?
Is it because I like to teach?
No way!

Maya Shalev (12)
JFS School, Harrow

Just Another Morning

Boom! Boom! Boom!
Here they come again into the classroom
Tables rumbling,
I start grumbling.

Students are so loud!
They're like the Brit Awards crowd
Why do they scream and shout?
Is that what they think school's all about?

Oh no! I forgot to mark their test,
It doesn't matter really, they don't even try their best.
They jump on top of me, like bombs from the sky,
Waiting for me to fall and die!

Urrghh! That Bobbi Brown,
He should be crowned the naughtiest kid in town!
Planning all the disturbing tricks,
In the playground bullying people,
Giving them mean punches and kicks.

Why couldn't they be more normal?
As well as dressing a bit more formal.
I am so tired from all the excuses they give me,
'My dog ate it' . . . 'It flew away' . . . 'My mum spilt her tea!'

That old boring staffroom
The staff sit there like a rusty broom.
How did I get into this job?
If anyone needs me, I'll be on my mob.

I'm going to have a nice cup of coffee,
Sit and relax, eating chocolate and toffee.

Georgia Meisel (11)
JFS School, Harrow

The Days Of Misery

When will these days of misery end?
Teaching and shouting,
My energy I spend,
Sitting at my desk, marking pages,
So I can earn these meagre wages.

Pupils are everywhere,
As numerous as ants,
Rushing and pushing,
Smash, bang, slant!

Hiding I try,
To my office I fly,
Real tears I cry,
Wishing the time would go by.

Boring biology,
Hateful history,
Why do I work here?
That's a mystery!

Ben Ezekiel (12)
JFS School, Harrow

Beggar

The people flow by,
Crash the money in his tin,
Quivering with a bottle of gin,
Cold as ice on the floor.

Click-clop the high-heels pass by,
Jackets and coats, red and white,
Sometimes the odd rustle or fight,
He walks all day, with only a little pay.

Past the pub and the museum,
He has no fear,
With a trickle of a tear,
Crackle, pop, New Year's passed by.

Laurence Greenberg (12)
JFS School, Harrow

Fantasy Fun Days At School!

Briiing!
Went my pink, fluffy alarm clock
It was the first day back
I grabbed a little snack
I ran as fast as lightning
To the bus stop

I waited and waited and waited
I jumped on the bus
Everyone made a humungous fuss

I ran to my locker right away
I wonder, do I have gym today?
First lesson, French
Then history
Oh, how I wish we could solve a mystery
I love school, it's soooo cool!

Katy Gale (11)
JFS School, Harrow

School

School is a place
School is a happy face
School is for friends
We don't want this day to end

School is a smile
School is wild
School is cool
Don't be fooled

Schooldays come by fast
So we need to make these days at school last
Be aware, you won't regret going to school
Because you will have to go to work!

Scott Krieger (11)
JFS School, Harrow

Narrated By Death

I saw him - the dark, solemn silhouette of desolation
He had caught my attention as I wandered aimlessly
Through my soupy swimming pool of unworthy and stale souls
I could smell his regret, his sins of the past
He grabs blindly at them, trying desperately to drag them
Onto the future and replay them
Swiping away the ingredient of a terrible deed
I stare towards his long, yet limp, feet, as they stumble
Across the cobblestone path of an anonymous location
I can hear his heart bleed
Can smell his need for my help and I am ready
The sky is hollow and grey, with a hard, stony face
And stabbing, rapier eyes
Though the man bites and clenches as he droops his head
He cannot reduce the rainfall of guilt that pelts ever harder
On his shoulders
The shower engulfs him and floods his heart -
He falls to his grazed knees and silently screams
His upper half and crumpled face falls forward
In a motion of thorough distress
A pool of damp, lush dissatisfaction
Leaks from his ever-descending soul
His soul is emptied and drifts in the form of fog towards the stale sky
I grasp it; my skeletal tendrils curl around it
Like a snake engulfing a helpless field mouse
I am satisfied.

Dylan Behr (11)
JFS School, Harrow

Why Bother Getting Up?

I wake up every morning
And in my head I can hear the sound
Of squealing children running around
All day long I hear,
'Ow!'
'Pick me, Miss!'
'No, pick me, Miss!'
And it drives me up the wall
So, why did I bother getting up?

The best time of the day, is break, by far
All the children out of my sight
Until I hear,
'You broke my toy!'
'No, you broke it!'
The children are fighting
And they're clearly not writing.

They come into class like monkeys in a zoo
All chatting away and thinking it's OK
The children may be young
But they're still not that dumb
To know to stop talking
I think I might just walk it
So, why do I bother getting up?

Matthew Newton (11)
JFS School, Harrow

It Doesn't Stop!

It's another year,
It's another week,
It's another day,
It's another hour
And it doesn't stop!

Blah, blah, blah, blah, blah,
That's all I ever hear,
From those annoying children,
The students are as wild as animals
And it doesn't stop!

My classes are so boring,
I would just be sitting there,
Fall asleep, even start snoring,
It's so annoying
And it doesn't stop!

The students are like screams,
Coming from a woman in trouble,
They are like bees,
That don't stop buzzing around your head
And it doesn't stop!

I just want the pain to end,
It's a nightmare marking work,
Reports over and over again!
There is not one peaceful day,
Something has to go wrong!
And it doesn't stop!

Monique Kaufman (12)
JFS School, Harrow

The Class Of Wild Dogs

I teach a class of wild dogs
Running all over the room,
They're as skilled as Mark Poom (Arsenal goalkeeper)
The pupils are like wild dogs
Chasing their prey
They have way more energy
Than a person whose hair is grey.

The only sounds I hear all day, are
Crash, bang, and zoom, zoom
And when the bell rings at the end of the day
The chaotic children never stop
All day, any day.

It's the first day back
From the summer holidays
Teaching the children
Is like teaching a bunch of animals
That never listen to you.

I don't really enjoy teaching
Or even going to school
I'd much rather stay at home all day
I can't be bothered to go to school really.

But I might get told off for it
Oh well, I might as well go
Do you think I should go, or not?

Marc Berman (11)
JFS School, Harrow

The Day Will Never End

The bell has rung
And I'm dreading the day,
There is nothing worse than teaching kids on a Monday,
The Year 7s are elephants, noisy and loud,
I'll have to give them detentions all round,
Now a coffee break,
Knock, knock, knock at the door
The inspector has come,
Oh, what joy, what fun!
I'll have to act like a perfect pupil at school,
I feel like I'm drowning in a swimming pool!
There are a few more hours left of the day, but they feel like years,
It's hard to stop myself from making rivers of tears,
In my last lesson, a girl named Jess, came up to me
And asked, 'Why are you so unhappy?'
I replied by saying, 'What are you talking about? I'm full of glee,
I teach English and DT!'
The day has ended, I scream and shout,
But I then realise I have to repeat my day tomorrow,
I become sad and fill with doubt.

Naomi Mendoza-Wolfson (11)
JFS School, Harrow

The Crystals In The Sky

As bright as twinkly crystals
Hanging from the ceiling,
Like a million blinking eyes
Watching over the world.
As white as tiny petals
That grow on every daisy,
Like thousands of people
Travelling the sky.
As tiny as a grain of sand
That lies on every beach,
As delicate as a tiny person
Like a flicker of a candle flame.
As dazzling as a light bulb's light
Sailing across a giant, black blanket,
As shining as a diamond ring,
That sits on someone's finger.
As dreamy as a Caramel Cream
Melting away in a little girl's hand,
Like a million souls drifting
Among each other,
In the sky.

Alice Ivell (12)
JFS School, Harrow

A Poem About A Poem

A poem does not have to rhyme
Well, not all the time
It can have alliteration
And must have punctuation.

A poem is amazing in every single way
Everyone should read one at least once a day
A poem should have verses and not paragraphs
And if you like a poem, you should read it to your class.

A poem is fantastic, it can make you laugh
You can even read a simple poem in the bath
Poems can be read on any random day
But this poem was written on a Wednesday.

A poem is exciting and makes your heart beat fast
A poem can be modern and can be from the past
A poem is fascinating for others to read
And when you write your own poem, you will be pleased.

To round off my poem, I would like to say a few words
A poem is like a peaceful bird
All poems can teach us many different skills
And some exciting poems can give us thrills!

Juliet Loumansky (12)
JFS School, Harrow

The Night Sky

Way, way, into the night,
All these beautiful stars so bright,
Gleaming away,
Nothing to say,
Oh, what a beautiful sight.

The sun went down hours ago,
Leaving behind a sparkling glow,
As I chill out,
I wonder in doubt,
If this will stay or go.

The stars are like crystals in the night sky,
Shining way up high,
How I can sit here,
With no fear,
With the brightness in my eye.

Now we go to the crescent moon so nice,
That is, of course, as quiet as mice,
As I look ahead,
Nothing looks dead,
I am amazed, to be precise.

Carly Wood (12)
JFS School, Harrow

My Amazing Grandpa!

My amazing grandpa,
The most supportive person ever,
Not afraid to joke, no never!

My amazing grandpa,
Always supported me in my time of need,
You see, it's a long story made short!

My amazing grandpa,
Helped me when my dad died,
So it was my time of grief!

My amazing grandpa,
This is my tribute for thee,
You know how much I love you and I can't repay you.

My amazing grandpa,
I could never and won't be as cheery,
But that is just your life's theory.

My amazing grandpa,
Now you've had a setback,
I will help thee, not just for you, but also me.

My amazing grandpa,
Although you lost a leg,
I couldn't live without helping you or I would just be mean!

My amazing grandpa,
You and I have a special bond
And no matter what we face, we'll stick together.

My amazing grandpa,
You and I will see everything through together,
With the help of the family.

You see, my amazing grandpa,
This is my special tribute to thee,
We will stick together!

Jonathan Asher Zealander (11)
JFS School, Harrow

The Mega Limerick

There once was a man called Lance,
Who wanted to learn to dance,
He flew up in the air,
Everyone would stare,
Then he went to France.

After that he went to Spain,
In a paper aeroplane,
When the plane made a crash,
It made such a bash,
Then he met up with Wayne.

Then he went to Chile
And met an old hillbilly,
He hit Lance round the head
And locked him in the shed,
That was the old hillbilly called Willy.

Then he went to Styke,
To buy a motorbike,
He called it rose,
Then hit his nose,
Then went on a hike.

Finally, Lance went home,
To find a dead gnome,
His wife smashed it,
Then she bashed it,
Now Lance is all alone.

Now he has a pet cat,
Wearing a funny hat,
He purred and purred,
Then ate a bird,
Finally, he hit it with a bat.

Charlie Appleby (12)
JFS School, Harrow

Bill And The Pasta Factory

Bill, a boy of ten, ate pasta every day,
No matter what, work, rest or play.
Pasta was like life and blood to him,
If he didn't eat it, he felt grim.

One day, he said, 'Pasta is like the sun,
It's like a hot dog in a bun,
Its texture is so nice
Especially with a bit of spice.'

Once he came back home,
No pasta to be found,
All the stores were shut,
His face was on the ground,
He walked with his heart in his hat,
Until he walked by the chef Franco Rozzetis Italian flat.

He looked at the house,
The door was ajar,
His heart was racing,
Pasta wasn't that far.

He slowly tiptoed into Franco's home,
He scanned the area, evidently he wasn't alone,
In front of him, was standing his best friend of all time,
A large bag of pasta, borrowing it would not be a crime.

Before he got out, clean and free,
He heard a door slam and before anyone could see,
He jumped into the nearby closet,
Which turned out to be a lovely factory.

Not a factory of chocolate,
Or one of cheese,
But one filled with his favourite things,
It was pasta, which gave him power,
He even grew wings!

Bill, a boy of ten, ate pasta every day,
No matter what work, rest or play,
Pasta was like life and blood to him,
If he didn't eat it, he felt grim.

Look at what pasta could do to a boy!

Jordan Mizrahi (12)
JFS School, Harrow

Day On A Farm

There are many animals on the farm
Some of which live in the barn

The cows eat all the grass
Whilst the cat breaks all the glass

Horses eating all the food
And the pigs are in a terrible mood

Billy the farmer is planting some seeds
Whilst his funny cousin was in Leeds

The potatoes were being dug up
Billy was drinking from a cup

The ducks were swimming in the lake
While the sheep were taking a break

Now it's the end of the day
Tomorrow is the first day of May.

Josh Frey (12)
JFS School, Harrow

What's The Point Of Going To School?

What's the point of going to school?
All you get is rule after rule
I want to learn and grow up smart
Yet all I want to do is PE and art

What's the point of going to school?
I like to run, not sit on my stool
Most teachers scream and shout
And point to the door and say, 'Out!'

What's the point of going to school?
Teachers and children can be very cruel
You wake up early and get home late
It's not ideal, it's far from great

What's the point of going to school?
The word on the street is, it isn't cool
One of the points is making friends
Sharing thoughts and starting new trends

I know the point of going to school
I don't want to end up like a fool
English, maths, history and art
Are most of the things that make me smart.

Natalie Sternberg (11)
JFS School, Harrow

Rachel's Garden

My favourite flower is the rose
A rose is very pretty
The soft rose reminds me of candyfloss
This pink flower is very shiny
My surname is Rose
And I enjoy seeing a glossy rose.

Yellow reminds me of the shimmering sun
Glowing in the sky.

The white flowers are like snowflakes
Falling from the sky
And children having snow fights.

Blue reminds me of the blue swishing waves of the sea
And children making sandcastles and having fun.

Orange reminds me of having ginger hair
And playing hairstyles on my accessory girl.

Black reminds me of being sad
Because it is a dull colour.

Green is like a Christmas tree
And bugs munching on green leaves.

Rachel Rose (12)
JFS School, Harrow

Seasons

Winter is full of snow and frost
White as the full, round moon
We get up in the dark each morning
And when school ends, it's dark again

In spring the flowers are starting to appear
Like little heads popping out from the dark earth
The happy robin starts hopping around
Butterflies come out from their cocoons

People leave behind their houses
And go out into the park to play

In summer, there's no one around
Except on the beach, where they'll be found
Children splishing and splashing in the sea
Like happy dolphins showing off to me

Autumn is next, after summer
The wind shakes the trees till the leaves settle down
They cover the path and crunch under our feet
And then it all starts again with . . . winter!

Tamara Azouri (12)
JFS School, Harrow

Deep Blue Ocean

(Inspired by the 2004 tsunami)

Deep blue sea - when I first saw you, I was petrified,
I thought you were going to swallow me up
With your powerful current,
But after a while, you gave me another impression,
You kept me calm and relaxed.

Deep blue sea - at first, your waves gave me a shock,
I thought you hated me and wanted to eat me,
With your mouth-eating waves,
But after a while, you quietened me down,
You soothed me with your sparkling looks.

Deep blue sea - I am with you always
And I am not scared of you now,
I will always be right under you,
Beside you, or however you describe it,
But I just wish my family could see me again.

Tamara Fox (11)
JFS School, Harrow

My First Haircut

My mummy and my daddy walk me in,
I hear all the people there, talking and talking,
I see the brush, the scissors and the hairdryer,
My daddy told me this was safe, what a liar!

My first haircut . . .

A lady sits me in a black metal chair,
Down to her toes was her hair,
You could hear her gum going *pop, pop,*
Whilst my hair went *chop, chop!*

My first haircut . . .
I look in front of me and I see my reflection,
Then I look beside me - a man with a bald section!
The long-haired lady takes off my black cape,
She blow-dries my hair while completely draped.

My first haircut . . .

Down below me was my chopped hair,
Now my head feels completely bare!
We walk out the salon altogether,
I'm not getting another haircut - *ever!*

Théa Marks (12)
JFS School, Harrow

I Can't Write A Poem!

I can't write a poem
Because it's tremendously hard
I hate thinking up a rhyming scheme
And making a theme.

I can't write a poem
Because I can't use onomatopoeia
Or homophones or similes
I hate poems, it's very hard

There once was a man from Peru
And he didn't know what to do
He thought for a long time
And decided to eat a lime
And then he had something to do.

Oh, a poem!
I just wrote a poem
With a rhyme scheme
And a very odd theme
I just wrote a poem!

Joel Anders (12)
JFS School, Harrow

Life

Life is something you should never forget
There is no point of letting it fade away
Because it will never come back once it's gone
Try to keep your life on track
It's not over yet.

Life can be happy
Don't let that go away
Spend time and be clappy
For time is running out, day by day

Be nice to others
Treat them with respect
Give everyone a chance
Treat your friends like brothers
Don't just give someone a horrid glance

Do things you have never done
Enjoy life, while you've got it
In the end it will turn out fun
You life isn't just a little bit of a run

Life will never end
Without a friend
So never pretend
Because life will never come to an unhappy end

People will always be there for you
You are not alone
Do not do bad things
So never ever postpone

It is always about the inside, not the out
Don't judge people on what they are all about
So, always be friendly and open a door
For life should be a wonderful opportunity, not war.

Joshua Battat (11)
JFS School, Harrow

Bank Robbery

First, there's the guard,
Sitting at his desk.
I pick up a rock and shatter a window,
It works, the guard has bolted to see what has happened.
I speed through the doors,
While the guard is checking the mess
And shoot up the steps, 83 floors.

I'm finally on floor 83,
The top floor of the building.
But I see a guard guarding a door,
Which is definitely the door to the vault.
He cradles an automatic rifle,
But I'm ready and prepared,
With a yell, I hurl my 6'2" body at him,
But he's a giant 6'8".
I send him flying and he drops his rifle
And goes speeding through the window,
He's got a 500m plus drop.

I kick open the door,
Rifle in my hand and my silenced pistol in my holster.
I stroll over to the vault,
There's a 14 digit code,
But I override the system.
I stuff all the trillions of dollars in my bag
And climb onto the roof
And throw myself off the top, opening my parachute as I go.
I'm well and truly battered,
But who said breaking into American National Bank was easy?
Zurich, here I come!

Yoni Greis (12)
JFS School, Harrow

At The Park, I Play My Part, All On A Summer's Day!

At the park,
I play my part,
I play on the swing,
I share the slide,
All on a summer's day.

At the park,
I play my part,
I play on the see-saw,
I share the house,
All on a summer's day.

At the park,
I play my part,
I play on the field,
I share the monkey bars,
All on a summer's day.

At the park,
I play my part,
I hear the school bell,
I go inside,
All on a summer's day.

Chloe Lasher (12)
JFS School, Harrow

The Four Seasons

Spring is meant to be joyful
This is what I think
Spring is colourful
Spring is nice
Spring is happy
And spring is when flowers bloom

Summer is meant to have lovely weather
This is what I think
Summer is hot
Summer is time to have cold food
In summer, it doesn't rain

Autumn is meant to be when leaves turn brown
This is what I think
Autumn is when trees lose their leaves
In autumn it rains
Autumn is cold

Winter is meant to be cold
This is what I think
Winter snows
Winter rains
Winter kills plants.

Joshua Davis (11)
JFS School, Harrow

Watching Your Life Pass Away

You are born one day,
In a warm and happy home,
With a warm and new feeling inside you,
With people all around you, watching you.

You are thinking,
Of how much you want to grow up
And be like those people,
Watching another person.

One year goes by,
Two years go by
And you are watching another person,
Watching your little sister.

One year goes by,
Two years go by,
You get so fed up of people watching you,
You watching other people
And you run away with a cold and empty feeling inside you.

One year goes by,
Two years go by,
Ten years go by
And you've got married, watching your own warm and happy home.

You have waved goodbye to your family,
As you watch them at their funerals
And you regret growing up, knowing that all you ever have done
Is watch other people
And you look back at the days when you were brand new
And you thought of how much you miss
Having that warm, new feeling inside you.

You have realised,
That your life was pointless,
Watching other people,
Watching your life pass away.

Yael Mahgerefteh (11)
JFS School, Harrow

Fireworks

The night was here and the time was right
It was November the 5th and it was Firework Night!
The children are here with sparklers in hand
People had come from all over the land

The clock's striking eight o'clock
And with a big bang, the fireworks are off
Rockets and Catherine wheels dominate the sky
In come the screamers and *whoosh!* Watch them fly!

Now it is still
I can feel the chill
Until next year, we'll meet again
My lovely, banging firework friend.

Jamie Gance (11)
JFS School, Harrow

The Magician

Emerging from the smoke,
A dark figure cloaked in blue,
A long black staff and a tall blue hat,
Astonished, I asked, 'Who are you?'
'The magician.'

He had a black, scraggly beard
And a huge, big wart on a long, thin nose,
He looked sad, depressed and glum
And in his right hand was a wilting rose,
The magician.

He shuffled along like a caterpillar,
He went to the gravestone, grim as can be
And knelt glumly and read the inscription,
Angry words formed on his lips,
'Go away! Let me be!' said he,
The magician.

Daniel Katz (12)
JFS School, Harrow

My Wine Cellars

I keep my old cellars cool and still,
Stacked high with great wooden casks,
To serve you up with great and good will,
With any drink you ask.

Ginger ale or pale ciders,
Specific and strong red wine,
Beer, enough for an army is here,
I promise mine does taste fine!

So, when you're feeling thirsty,
Please, do drop in for the night,
We'll sing lusty songs, words right or wrong,
Finish keg after keg, walk with wobbly legs,
Back to our beds, after barrels of beer,
Till the morn sun comes up
And the heat is here, saying, 'Back to work! Forget last night!
Your hangover's here, it's out of sight!'

Noam Barkany (12)
JFS School, Harrow

The Swing

In the gusting winds,
The moon gazes down upon the land.
Back and forth upon my swing,
As the sun turns to slumber.
The night screams its terrible thunder
And there I am, all alone,
Back and forth upon my swing.
The grass stand up as if to sing,
The trees are as silent as a rock.
The swing's rust creaks, like a door,
On its last day.
But nothing matters when you're all alone,
Swinging back and forth upon my swing.

Joel Turner (12)
JFS School, Harrow

Sweets

Boiled, chewy, sticky and yummy,
They completely fill my tummy,
They rot my teeth,
But never give me grief.

Sweets, sweets, sweets.

I wish I could swim in a sweet filled pool,
Or be allowed to eat sweets in school,
When I eat sweets, I fall into a fabulous dream,
They look as good as they taste, as it might seem.

Sweets, sweets, sweets.

Sweet or sour in my mouth,
You can find them, north or south,
They always have an amazing taste,
So never let them go to waste!

Sweets, sweets, sweets.

Emily Caplan (11)
JFS School, Harrow

Dis Dark World

Dis dark world, rainin' fru da days and da night,
Da col' win bites.
Many people on da streets, but we can't see eachovah,
Like we invisible walkin' past one anovah.
Dirty grey ground and dark cloudy skies,
We all seem to fink it's alright to tell lies.
No troof! No values!
Our souls are lost, dey need to be rescued.

Nebula Hart-Leverton (12)
JFS School, Harrow

Scared Of The Dark

As she walked through the dark,
She suddenly saw a shining spark.

As glittery as a fairy's wing
And then she heard a high-pitched *ping!*

It touched the ground and then it shook
Was it alive? She wouldn't look.

She screamed for help, but no one came
When then she heard someone shout her name.

'*Georgia, come here!*'
She wouldn't answer and shivered with fear.

As it came nearer and nearer
It all started to become much clearer . . .

This was all a dream
And there was never a scream.

Not even a shining light
It was just her mother saying goodnight!

Courtney Freeman (12)
JFS School, Harrow

The Smile

The smile is a special feature,
The smile lies above the chin,
The smile makes me happy,
The smile makes me grin.

The smile is a hyena,
The smile is a wish,
The smile is a blooming flower,
The smile is a kiss.

The smile comes from the heart,
The smile spreads across your face,
The smile makes you feel warm,
The smile can never be out of place.

The smile is like a rainbow,
The smile is like a star,
The smile is always there for you,
The smile will travel far.

The smile makes you happy,
The smile is in your eyes,
The smile is so truthful,
The smile never lies.

Lucy Levy (12)
JFS School, Harrow

Seasons

I love the seasons,
Summer, autumn, winter and spring
For many different reasons.

In summer I see the ducks swimming on the lake,
I often sit and watch them
Whilst drinking tea and eating cake.
The sailing boats go floating by,
Who wouldn't like a day like that?
Not I!
In summer it makes me hot,
So I walk to the shops and buy a Jelly Tot.

In autumn I love to kick the leaves
Dressed in my cosy top with the long sleeves.
The colder weather is coming nearer
And the air is becoming less clearer,
Filled with rain and dust and fog.
I walk in the icy park, with Princess, my pet dog.
Autumn is cold,
My dad's head is red because it is bald.

In winter the lake freezes over
And everything dies, including the grass and the clover.
The snow falls think of the ground
And when I walk, my footsteps make no sound.
Winter makes me freezing,
I stay at home doing nothing
And my brother starts teasing.

When winter goes, along comes spring,
It is such a nice season, it makes me sing.
Spring makes me warm, so I go to the park,
The next morning I woke up and noticed a bad mark.
All four seasons come and go,
Summer, autumn, winter and spring,
All in a row.

Talia Golan (11)
JFS School, Harrow

A Rider In The Night

At the dead of night,
When the clouds grew still
And the trees rippled and shook,
A man came a-riding.

He came, draped in black,
His hands a glove of scars,
His red-rimmed eyes shone in the night sky,
His dull grey teeth blended into the darkness.

The shimmering crescent moon loomed over him,
He rode on as fast as he could,
Ignoring the sharp vines scratching against his face,
Ignoring the excruciating pain.

His horse shivered in the cold night,
The wind screamed out,
He and his equine companion trudged slowly forward,
In the damp, freezing night.

Leaves fell from the thin, stick-like trees
And snowed down on them,
Covering them,
Showering them with the decaying mould.

The wind began to quieten,
From a scream to a harsh whisper
And then, at last, the man collapsed from his horse,
Not to ride again.

At the dead of night,
When the clouds grew still
And the trees rippled and shook,
A man came a-riding . . .

Jack Prevezer (11)
JFS School, Harrow

The Seasons

Autumn
Red leaves,
Yellow leaves,
Tumbling down.
Bare trees,
Naked trees,
Standing silent; alone.
Paw prints,
Small and large,
Heavy and soft,
Clawed and not.
This is autumn,
The best time of year.

Winter
No leaves,
Naked trees,
Standing alone.
Soft snow,
Deep snow,
Burying grass.
White everywhere,
This is winter,
The cold time of year.

Spring
Cherry blossom,
Orange blossom,
Floating down.
Tall trees,
Coloured trees,
Standing stately; a crowd.
Laughter and song; petals,
For this is spring,
The happy time of year.

Summer
Green leaves,
Red leaves,
Held up high.
Wide trees,
Fruitful trees,
Standing colourful; a forest.
Orchards;
Large and small,
Fruitful, fruitless,
Colourful and drab.
This is summer,
The tasteful time of year.

Joe Solomons (12)
JFS School, Harrow

Time

Tick-tock, tick-tock
The clock will sometime have to stop
Tick-tock, tick-tock
Round and round it goes
Tick-tock, tick-tock
And the day passes by
Tick-tock, tick-tock
Do not waste your time
Tick-tock, tick-tock
The clock is going to stop
Tick-tock, tick-tock
Your time has nearly run out
Tick-tock, tick-tock
The clock is going to crash
Tick-tock, tick-tock
The clock has crashed
Tick-tock, tick-tock
You have now passed away.

Joe Botchin (11)
JFS School, Harrow

Colours

The world is a rainbow filled with many faces
All of which belong to different races
This causes problems, as we all know
So why can't every colour live together and flow?

Amil is Asian with skin that is brown
Lots of people look at him and frown
This makes him red, as angry as a bear
Who has been locked in a cage, with nobody to care

Safidi is African with skin that is black
Every day she walks miles, with the sun beating on her back
This makes her feel pink, as sore as a heart
That has been hurt and broken apart

Maya is a Jew with skin that is white
People don't like her, as she prays every night
This makes her feel blue, as sad as a child
Who gets pushed and shoved
All she wants is to be loved

The world is a rainbow filled with many faces
Now let's try to prevent these sorts of cases.

Jodi Sampson (12)
JFS School, Harrow

The New Girl, Me . . .

Pale face and dull brown hair,
Weird, sad, creepy, mad,
Sitting on her shoulders, bare.

Spotty nose and a double chin,
Weird, sad, creepy, mad,
A tatty shirt which smelt of gin.

Frowning with solemn eyes,
Weird, sad, creepy, mad,
The kind of look when someone dies.

Her name is Susan, she is ten,
Weird, sad, creepy, mad,
Miss Tee says again and again.

But do they care, I don't think so,
Weird, sad, creepy, mad,
They care enough to snigger though.

My name is Susan, I am ten,
I'm weird, sad, creepy, mad,
Miss Tee says again and again.

But do they care? I don't think so,
I'm weird, sad, creepy, mad
They care enough to bully though.

Emily Grosswald (12)
JFS School, Harrow

The Stray Cat

I am a stray cat strolling down the road,
On the way, I spot a guy carrying a load.
He stares at me, tearfully eyed,
He looks at me like I'm deprived.

He picks me up and strokes me with care
And hugs me gently, as if cuddling a bear.
He looks at me in a happy mode,
I am a stray cat strolling down the road.

I am a stray cat strolling down the street,
Scruffy and lost, staring at people's feet.
I pause at the corner, feeling terribly sad,
The happy people make me jealous and mad.

I also pass cats, but they're groomed and neat,
I am a stray cat, strolling down the street.

Gina Josephs (12)
JFS School, Harrow

A Falling Star

There is one star in the sky,
One shining star, oh my, oh my,
It looks like a light bulb,
One light bulb in the sky.

Everyone is looking at this
Extraordinary glow,
Even the baby with the
Bright blue bow.

I think that it is falling,
Coming to me,
I fear the worst, because
I can see . . .

It has fallen on me!

Rachael Simons (11)
JFS School, Harrow

Sunrise

The sun slides
Into view;
Colours scattered,
Clouds askew.

Shining grass,
Shimmering sky;
Something to
Catch your eye.

Rub my eyes,
Jump out of bed;
Lots to be seen;
None to be said.

Orange skies,
Turn to blue.
Into the day;
Lots to do.

Natalie Rose (11)
JFS School, Harrow

Sunset

Orange, yellow and red
As we get ready for bed
The sun is sleepy
The moon is awake

The sea is calm
And will not harm
Across the horizon
The sun will set.

Phoebe Salter (11)
JFS School, Harrow

My Football Poem

Football is my favourite sport and I'd just like to mention
When I watch a match, I can feel excitement and tension
The players in the dressing room, are quivering with nerves
Waiting to go out on the green, grassy turf

The teams run through the tunnel, like an army going to war
Determined to be the ones to score
The fans are all praying that their team will win
They scream, they shout, they cheer, they sing

The whistle blows, the game starts
The winger's with the ball, around the players he darts
He keeps on going, without a challenge
Defenders try to stop him, but he's hard to manage

He's still got the ball and he crosses to a mate
Who controls it to the ground, his skill is great
He turns around and the fans all roar
He pulls his leg back, he's ready to *score!*

It's hit the back of the net, that powerful shot
The keeper is left standing - the shot was too hot
The players and fans are celebrating, with their hands in the air
The opposition are amazed, they can only stare

Ninety minutes is up, it's the end of the game
The winners are happy, the losers in shame
The losing team are no longer excited
But the team that were winners, are very delighted!

Oliver Hart (12)
JFS School, Harrow

My Dog, Ben

We open the cage and he looks scared and shy,
He walks to the corner and closes his eyes.
Tamara runs over to follow him,
She doesn't know that he wants to be alone.

He's suddenly awake and barking out loud,
I think, for once, he is having some fun.
He jumps on my chest and licks my face,
I throw him his toy bun
And he jumps like crazy,
I love my dog, but he loves his toy bun.

We now spend every second together,
Playing or walking, whatever it is,
He is specially mine.
My own special friend,
I don't need anyone else, because I have my dog, Ben.

He sleeps on the floor,
Right next to my bed.
He smiles up at me when I look down,
We never frown,
Or fight or shout,
Because we love each other and that's what matters.

Every morning, when I wake up, Ben is there,
But just this morning, after exactly five years with each other,
Little Ben isn't there, I now feel alone,
I loved Ben and I know he loved me!

Alana Robinson (11)
JFS School, Harrow

Nature And Wildlife

Butterflies fly like planes in the air
Flowers start to grow like a hawk's glare
A lion sits on a dirty rock
But not the mouse that the world forgot

A thunderstorm strikes over the beach
As waves come crashing like a white sheet
Fish start to swim as they move their fins
But when a net comes they'll be put in tins

Monkeys swing from vine to vine
Then the sun begins to shine
As the cheetah runs by
Birds flap their wings and hit the sky

Minute by minute, day by day
Nature's music starts to play
The circle of nature starts again
And trees start to produce oxygen.

Zack Turofsky (11)
JFS School, Harrow

It's Not True

Everybody says it's true
But it's really not
Everybody says it's true
Honestly, it's not

Everybody laughs at it
It makes me really mad
Everybody laughs at it
It makes me kind of sad

Everybody sneers and leers
It sends my eyes to tears
Everybody sneers and leers
Even all my peers.

I want to be a normal kid
Just like all the rest
I want to be a normal kid
So I can get some rest.

David Schogger (12)
JFS School, Harrow

My Bedroom

I'm going to talk about my bedroom
And what's in it, like my bed.
With the softest duvet and a colourful sheet
Of yellow, blue and red.

I also have a great big wardrobe,
With handles as big as your face!
My trousers, T-shirts, underwear and shorts,
My wardrobe's their hiding place.

I also have a convenient desk,
Its colour, a midnight black.
Next to it lies my comfy chair,
With a soft, blue, bouncy back.

Above my desk are some bookshelves,
With books by Charles Dickens
And stories like The Hobbit, The Borrowers too
And characters from humans to chickens.

So, that's a description of my room,
From wall to ceiling to floor.
It's also the end of my poem, so *bye!*
Now, let me show you the door.

Harry Stern (12)
JFS School, Harrow

The Monster

There's a monster walking down the street
It's looking kind of hairy,
It is as hairy as my dad's feet
And let's not forget, it's scary.

There's a monster walking down the street
It's laugh is grotesque and aches your ears
The sound is as squeaky as a door,
The monster's coming near, that's what I fear.

There's a monster near my house,
It's coming closer and closer,
The thing jumps up at my window,
It's like a piece of bread jumping out of a toaster.

There's a monster knocking at my door,
It won't stop,
The knocking's getting louder and worse,
I'm so scared, I feel like I'm going to pop.

There's a monster inside my house,
Chasing round the house to find me,
All you can hear is me screaming like a mouse,
I'm going crazy.

There's a monster and I'm in his tummy,
All I can see are horses floating around,
I'm sure that wasn't yummy!

Gabrielle Morris (11)
JFS School, Harrow

My Ordinary Day Went On!

6.30 came quick
And the snooze button wouldn't flick
I rolled over right, left, right
When my dad came in, oh, what a fright
And my ordinary day went on!

All lessons were so boring
The boy next to me was snoring
My marks were so bad in my tests
Teachers, such pests
And my ordinary day went on!

PE time was now here
They might even tell us to stand on our ear!
Getting dressed back is a pain
My friends, they go insane
And my ordinary day went on!

Home was round the corner
Mum was still in the sauna
But big sis was still eating
And dad was in a meeting
And my ordinary day went on!

Homework needs to be done
While I sing my favourite song in a hum
Getting ready for bed
My dog still wanting to play dead
I was now in a deep sleep
And my ordinary day had finished.

Jessica Lee (11)
JFS School, Harrow

I Can't Write A Poem

I can't write a poem,
Forget it, I give up,
I'm half asleep,
The harder I try, my brain will soon pop!
I can't be bothered,
I lost my pen,
It's just impossible to finish this in ten!

I try and I try,
But it doesn't seem to work,
Whatever am I going to do?
My brain is starting to hurt,
I just don't understand,
Why can't I do this?
My teacher will shout!
There she is,
Just sitting there, eating a trout.
It's as hard as equations,
It's has hard as a rock,
The clock is standing there saying, *tick-tock, tick-tock.*

What? Time's up!
Look at me, I have done nothing!
Oh no, hide me, she's coming!
Wait? You liked that? Really? No kidding!
You just helped me write my first poem!

Asaf Gomes De Mesquita (12)
JFS School, Harrow

Animals

Snakes are slithery,
Pigs are a misery,
Giraffes are taller,
Ants are smaller.

Camels have two humps,
Frogs have long jumps,
Chickens lay big eggs,
Storks have long legs.

A doe and a deer
Running away from fear,
A fox chasing after them,
Forgetting about his career.

A cheetah speeding fast,
Forgetting that it wouldn't last,
Its legs are a rocket,
Like they were plugged into a socket.

An external skeleton spider,
Climbing higher and higher,
They're munching on a grebe,
Just about to finish their web.

A snail has a shell,
Which has a very distinctive smell,
A horse has a long face,
Which means it must always be in disgrace.

A lion munches on meat,
Forgetting about the heat,
A goat gobbles on grass,
Misplacing a necklace made out of brass.

A human is reading this poem,
Having a laugh and having fun,
But with animals in the poem,
The fun has just begun.

Joshua Klinger (11)
JFS School, Harrow

War

A cold day,
A silent night,
A knock on the door,
Get as far away . . .
I flee . . .
A scream, a gunshot,
Caught,
They take me,
A shower,
It's only a shower,
That's what they say,
Gas,
All around me,
The door,
It opens,
I run,
A gun,
It shoots,
I fall,
I see them,
My mother,
My father,
Dead.
War?
This is not war,
This is madness,
Massacre,
No pride,
No glory,
Only death.

Zac Rubin (12)
JFS School, Harrow

The Monster

It sneaks through the forests
And creeps in your house
You start to taste a smell.

You hear a creak
And suddenly wake up
You creep into the dining room.

There it is
Standing right there
You think you're going to die.

What shall you do?
Should you stay there?
Should you run?

You run to your room
And get the gun
You get ready.

You get the bullet
And put it in
You shoot.

So that was the end of the monster
But did it really die?
All they heard the monster say was
'I guess this is goodbye!'

Brandon Sassoon (11)
JFS School, Harrow

The Nerd In Our Class

In our class, there is a nerd,
In his spare time he plays with his bird,
He wears big, bright glasses
And we sit giggling in classes.

The nerd in our class
Eats lots of grass
He drinks warm milk
And his pyjamas are silk.

In our class, the nerd always has a long face,
Only because he wants to play kiss-chase,
When he sings we cover our ears,
When he stops, we all shout, 'Cheers!'

In our class, I sit next to him,
Unfortunately, he is ever so dim.
He always uses fish shampoo
And makes noises when he needs the loo!

You now know enough about our not-so-special friend,
Now luckily, this poem has come to an end!

Beth Greene (12)
JFS School, Harrow

The Moonlight

The moonlight shone on the summer green,
As the lightless breeze flew across the sea,
But then I saw something strange and black,
A long, shiny shadow running with ease,
Grey, black and fierce, a wolf hunting its prey,
Running faster and faster to catch it in his claws.

It ran up a hill, into the pale moonlight
And then we saw his shiny bright eyes
As he stood there, looking up with pride
He howled at the moonlight, oh, what a sight
The moonlight shone on the summer green,
As the delicate breeze flew away from me.

Higher and higher up to the starlit sky,
Until it was vanished up into the darkness
And then, when it was gone, I stopped and thought
And decided to end with a song at midnight,
The song travelled far and wide
Until the whole world could hear my cry
And the I stopped, stood and listened
And then I heard a howl filled with pride.

Rachel Jacobs (12)
JFS School, Harrow

True Love Has Gone

My true love is dead
I am alone, alone, alone
When will I find the right one again, again, again?
When will I find true happiness?
My broken heart is just like stone
Hard and cold
I should just die and be alone, alone, alone
For all eternity, with no one by my side
I am the saddest person in the whole galaxy
Who is there for me to accept my miserable self?
Not me, not no one
Again and again, I'm thinking
Can someone just shoot me?
But no one will
So, I say to myself, *I'm alone again with my reckless old self*
Just like the moon, all by itself
No place to go, I'm so lost
Farewell my true love, we will meet again one day, one day
Like the stars in the sky, reuniting together once again, again, again.

Aaron Ibrahim (12)
JFS School, Harrow

The Windows To The Soul

The eyes are recognised as the windows to the soul
So when you look into my eyes, what do you see?

A soul passionate with music and art
A stone-cold, self-centred heart,
A pathetic, submissive loser,
A mischievous, deceitful liar,
A big-headed, effortless successor
Who has a life where she is always a winner,
A spiritually intact young Christian,
An outcast, who doesn't fit in.

These are the opinions you may have of me,
But each of these characteristics disenfranchises me.
Ignore my common, ebony brown eye colour,
Don't characterise me as another.
I am a blend, who wants to be known,
To be accepted, not left on my own.

And so again, I ask,
When you look into my eyes, what do you see?
A Christian intending to inspire,
A young woman,
Me.

Valentina Okolo (15)
La Sainte Union Convent School, London

Xhuxhied

Coral stains the dress,
And porcelain fingers call him.

Black on white
White on black
Sere kisses . . . Carmine singeing the room

But, the laced love was meant for two.
And the Moor's chair is too old, too weak, to lust

Over.

And so, rocking tarsia
Bed,
Floor,
And girl
Are no more.

The man is the head.
And the woman is there to turn that head.

Clarissa Pabi (17)
La Sainte Union Convent School, London

My Vision Of The Future . . . 3008

In the year 3008, there will be . . .
No prime minister because . . .
Aliens will take over our planet.

Aliens are good because . . .
They have stopped gun crime . . .
And there are no wars because . . .
Everyone has chilled.

In the year 3008, there will be . . .
No poverty and all will be cared for . . .
There will be no hunger . . .
And all have homes.

There will be no schools in the year 3008 . . .
Because teachers will teach you at your home . . .
Because pupils don't go to school . . .
So everyone will be educated.

Joseph Jones
Lilian Bayliss Technology School, London

Looking Out My Window

I look out my window and see
An electronic bee
All the animals are extinct.

Looking out my window I see
Colourful flying cars
And delicious epitome chocolate bars.

Looking out my window I see
More bright green trees
Full of wonderful leaves.

Looking out the window I see
A peaceful community
And androids selling trees.

Looking out my window I see
My future to be.

Shaira Rahman (12)
Lilian Bayliss Technology School, London

If I Could Change The Future

If I could change the future,
Then what would I do?
Change war and poverty,
Change me and you.

If I could change the future,
Then what will there be?
Space cars, hover scooters,
Flying cups of tea.

If I could change the future,
Then what colour would it be?
Pink, gold or silver,
Or different shades of green.

If I could change the future,
Then how many races of life would there be?
Animals, robots, androids,
Everyone like me.

If I could change the future,
Then how many languages would we speak?
1,000, 2,000, 3,000,
As many as you could shriek.

If I want to change the future,
Then it can't just be me,
We all need to help each other,
To make it what we want it to be.

Leia Bagge (12)
Lilian Bayliss Technology School, London

My Future

What would it be like,
If the world was upside down?
What would it be like,
If there were androids round the town?

If I could change the world,
I'd make speaking dictionaries,
If I could change the world,
I'd make huge android canaries.

If I could form tall buildings,
I would make them high and tilt,
If I could form tall buildings,
I'd build it far away from silt.

But how am I able to build these things,
With only my two human hands?
For I haven't got any wings
And fly all over the lands.

If I could change the future,
I would mix the Earth with Mars,
But how on earth do we get there?
Oh yes! On rocket cars!

If I could transform humans,
I'd change them how they want to be,
With loads of different fonts
And different opportunities.

Stephanie Da Silva (13)
Lilian Bayliss Technology School, London

My Vision Of The World In 3008

Some things can be better
Than it is today
But then again, if something's changed
Then it might not be the same

If everything changed
The world would be dull
Everything silver with no colours
Think of how boring it would be

We'd go to school in space pods
Or maybe even a shuttle car
There's no way we'd be able to walk
We'd be floating all over the place

Tall, silver buildings
Growing to the sky
Just looking out the window would be weird
With all the space pods whizzing around

I could have an android
That would do anything I say
It would be in all my lessons
That I wouldn't be in today

We'd have to eat our food through straws
Not eating anything solid
If we ate like we did today
It would go everywhere

So, if you see where I'm coming from
Some things would be great
Like going to school in space pods
But that just wouldn't be the same.

Shannon Johnson (12)
Lilian Bayliss Technology School, London

Teardrops

Surrounding my life,
Is a whole lot of stress
And in this sad poem,
I am about to express!

My heart tore apart,
When my mum left me
And in my clogged mind,
She is all I can see.

The last words she said,
'Like father, like son;'
I think, *is it true?*
Oh dear, I miss my mum!

She cooked and she cleaned
And made my lunch nice,
Ever since my dad took over,
We have only had cold rice.

I have made new friends,
Julius and Charmain,
They are very nice people,
But ever so tame!

On 56 Croxley Street,
Lay a haunted house there,
We always end up on Croxley,
Enter the house, we never dare!

At the end of the day,
That is my life,
I hope I could get rid of
The pain and the strife.

Errol Moore-Amaadzie (13)
Rutlish School, Merton

A Lonely Kiss Of Sadness

Standing in front of the dancing flames,
I feel the warmth of the burning fire,
The wind rushes past me like a stampede of poltergeists,
When the day of which the fire blew out the sadness blew in,
The thunderous arguments of male and female
Made little waterfalls in my soulless eyes.

On 72 Boxley Hill, one death led to another,
The knife that slit her throat into a million memories
Is still fixed into my mind,
Bullying is another when you have to run for your life,
Tanker and Ryan, the teenaged bullies,
Always starting the same waterfalls on my cracked face.

Coming home from the drowning rain
I wish that my beautiful mother never had to go,
Hardly walking on the junk-filled carpet and dirty cups,
I thought of what it would be like to die,
As china cups crack leaving dark red lines,
I hoped my dad would be home later,
Every day my father comes back,
The sadness and trauma starts again.

Running to bed, I snuggle up tight in my painful, springed bed,
A lonely wind kisses my cheeks; I hope the sadness would stop,
Oh why, oh why, did this ever happen?
I feel like I want to take on suicide,
In the morning, my father tells a diabolical story
About a man that killed his wife and how he hanged himself after,
I wonder if the silent rope still swings
On the top of the chamber of stairs.

At 54 Boxley Hill, the rope awaits its new victim,
Its staring at me, as I step up onto the chamber of stairs,
The lonely wind kisses my cheeks for one last time,
Holding the bloody rope, I jump,

Arrrrrccc, arrrrcccc!
The only sound that was left,
The mysterious crows on the top of the roof
Flying away, up to the sky.

Kieran Hashmi (13)
Rutlish School, Merton

Haunted House Poem

In an old haunted house
Where there's nothing but a mouse
And insects and rats
And in the basement, bats
You might hear a bang
And also a clang
At the rattle of chains
Covering an engineer of trains
But dead and as a ghost
Who haunts the house
And feeds on the rats and mice
Whoever comes to the door
Is dinner, eaten with a roar
Until one day, when a gang of three come
And see him coming through the post hole
And they ran, ran, ran away
But the ghost hears them talk
Buddy's the name, as they walk
Buddy, I will see you again
But then you will be dinner
And I will be the winner.

Stephen Arnold (13)
Rutlish School, Merton

Hassle-free World

I wish I was in a hassle-free world,
Everyone would be happy,
No wars, no gangs, no fights, just *love*

Everyone would forgive each other
And everyone would have a home,
No rich, no poor, no hatred, just *love*

Every child has the right to be heard,
Their opinions taken into account,
No discrimination, no injustice, no bigotry, just *love*

The whole world is at peace,
Countries will help each other,
No tax, no prejudice, no favouritism, just *love*

I believe in a place like this,
We all could make the change
And make the world hassle-free.

Liam Rhys Davies (12)
Rutlish School, Merton

Climate Change

I got an important message to say,
About a thing called climate change.

We don't want the winters to change into summer,
Or the summer to turn into the cold and bitter winter,
So do something about it, you can help,
So please, please recycle and get on a bicycle.

If you do one simple thing like recycle,
Or get on a bicycle, you can change the world.

Richard David Woolland (12)
Rutlish School, Merton

War - Haikus

War is what I am,
There is innocent bloodshed,
Why must there be war?

Ghosts of my soldiers,
Have to fight a losing war,
Why must soldiers die?

Why would I fight war?
I will fight for the country,
I will be a hero

Always I will fight,
I will bleed for my country,
I fight to the death!

Innocents will die,
I feel their blood on my hands,
That's why I will fight.

Kaseem Miah (12)
Rutlish School, Merton

Earth Suffers - Haiku

I'm burning like Hell,
I'm rotting spots of rubbish,
My blood boils as well.

Humza Javaid Sarwar (12)
Rutlish School, Merton

The Journey - On My Trek For Water

The dusty path stretched for miles,
On my trek for water,
I walked with others on my quest,
On my trek for water,
Bare-footed, stones hurting my feet,
On my trek for water,
The sun was hot and high in the sky,
On my trek for water,
Balancing a jar on my head,
On my trek for water,
Two empty cans in each hand,
On my trek for water,
Mile after mile, stretches of sand,
On my trek for water,
On the horizon water flooding the land,
On my trek for water,
Flooding the land, I feel glad!
On my trek for water,
I fill my vessels with precious liquid,
I have reached my trek for water,
Now, which way is home? Where do I roam?
Back from my trek for water,
We wash, we cook, we clean, we drink,
Now we have fresh water.

Harvey Hands-Heart (13)
Rutlish School, Merton

The Minotaur

There once was a Minotaur, strong, great and bold
And many legends about him were told.
His muscles rippled in his dirt-brown coat,
He could fight, talk and even float.

His horns were saffron, sharp and tough,
His blood-red eyes suited for spotting the rough.
His hands ready to rip and tear
And his dripping fangs itching to scare.

In the jet-black dark, awoken was this beast
And off he loped, down the rocky cliffs, for a meat feast.
His tongue craved blood, his teeth asked for man
And he ate little children as much as one can.

The village people had endured this all,
Till they grew angry and gathered in a hall.
'What shall we do about this foul sin?
It's not some rubbish we can throw in the bin!'

'Call for a hero!' the mayor said,
'One you can strike a Minotaur dead!'
The people summoned him with much haste,
To put this being to bloody waste.

Clad in armour with a naked sword at his belt,
His cloak was a frost wolf's pelt.
Gold and riches they promised to pay,
The brave barbarian Prince Kay.

To the maw of the hellhole did Kay go,
Whether he would return, he did not know.
'Die!' Kay screamed and the beast saw,
A great sword: then the Minotaur knew no more.

Daniel Owusu (13)
Rutlish School, Merton

Home, Or No Home!

I have no house,
I have no home,
(Not even a garden)
For a mouse,
Or a garden gnome.

I live in Nairobi, in Kenya,
Where there is war and famine,
Where they go and send ya,
To no hospital with medicine.

Help me, for I need it!
My life has badly started,
I don't like my life one bit,
I am good-hearted.

My parents and siblings died,
So we were sadly parted!
I have really tried . . .
To get my life newly started!

I hate my horrible, terrible life,
It is really, truly dangerous,
But when I might get stabbed with a knife,
At least I'll go to Heaven, which is really vigorous!

I'm really, really poor,
I don't have to tell you more,
I'm so hungry I could eat a boar!
Being happy is what I adore!

If you help me,
I will be grateful
And I will be safe,
I'll never be hateful.

Home or no home,
I'll finally be safe in every way,
With no garden gnome,
I didn't want one anyway!

Hugh Evbuomwan (13)
Rutlish School, Merton

Notions Of Life

Cell particles hold pocketfuls of mysteries
Tears contain waterfalls of stories
Heartbeats code minutes of existence
Wombs guard puzzled imminent creatures
Eyes embrace daydreamed animations
A gasp motions legendary moments
Obscure pattering feet pave prologue beginnings
Tiny fingertips clench designed craftsmanship
Luscious vivacity screams into familiar trees
Articulate whispers present physical features
Narrated memories birth a mouthful of laughter
Dangerous elements survive spirited situations
Colourful unction beautifies sacred roles
Distributed oxygen digests mortality
Specified uniform rejects reality
Unmanning scribbles mould authenticity
Pessimistic tongues cripples hopeful Pandora boxes
Daring exceptions retrieve stolen changes
Previous experiences cannot refuse individuality
A baby's temptations escapes wisdom's mockery
Melting cries remember internal innocence
Pure mischief bursts repressive maintenance
Pulsating actions build insightful bridges
The original artist rejoices at forgiving generations
Dancing signs of father and mother reconciliation
Erase dull expressions of Mona Lisa smiles
Open to an exaggerated modernised version
Running around in squares rather than circles
Secular perfectionists forget he never made anything straight
Pinched, dimpled cheeks slow down the maturity date!

Victoria Awosode (17)
St Francis Xavier Sixth Form College, London

Crimson Fantasy

Amidst the eclectic hallucinations of she-roar,
Or neurotic illusions as protector of her fortress, she
Hovers in-between intrinsic space whilst abiding in the world below -
Merely mortal
She solicits the authority of natural elements
Unnatural inhales of fantasy
Naturalist authorisation to exhibit the affects
And as she vomits details of dreams
She prohibits the possibility of sanity
Rather concentrates the notion of eternal intoxication
Whilst unbeknownst to her
He seizes shadows of the former self
Releasing it to float amidst the stronghold of his fists, she is
Transformed
Reborn - erupted and like lather moulded
Allowed to settle until her discolourment
Is nor more recognisable to the common eye
Not to the eye which once depicted 'common' as submittance
And so, dusted purple and blue
She wanders in the mist of an eclipse
And fantasises of an apocalyptic epic where she -
Receives is judged on endurement
Flaws unattainable, rather intolerable to testosterone
Prone to abhor -
Black
And as mahogany sees through her eyes, her nose, her lips
She floats into a galaxy of gold
And struggles to patch her scattered cloud
Into him never able to connect him together,
Repelled by black holes of insignificant matter . . . it matters as
Her almost - instincts shackle her below her natural order
Although her passport is invalid
Escape translates to irrationality and kaleidoscopes define pain
Love is her battlefield and she unknowingly is the foe
But glazed with crimson fear, how can she know?

Debbie Bankole (17)
St Francis Xavier Sixth Form College, London

In Search Of . . .

Unanswered questions
That stand the test of time
Maybe in the next life
I'll have someone to call mine.
In this crazy journey called life,
My chosen place
Has no resting destination.
I need to find the pace
To rest this ailing heart,
Going round in circles
Retracing my footsteps
I'm trapped in this cycle
Of understood misconceptions
I'm travelling through emotions
Of distant relations
I choose to accept change
So I can paint the image
Of what is perfect
But what is perfect?
Can the dream in front of me
Be so real?
Or is the jagged outline
Crumbling to my feet
The symbols and signs
All around me
Unravelling the gift he was to me.
Recreating the retrospective
Learning to *let* go
Learning to *love* myself
In search of . . . *you.*

Marion Osieyo (17)
St Francis Xavier Sixth Form College, London

Bullying

They're bitching me, kicking me, literally hitting me,
Cowardly, sitting me here
The chicken me, inner me, sinfully, part of me,
Fearfully, sits in the chair
I'm carefully, tearfully, they don't see tears from me
They all just laugh at me, half of me
Wants to be free from this misery
That part of me, can't be, 'cause I'm sitting shakily,
Making me believe that I should be hating me,
Hating me, hating me,
Forget them, I hate them back!
They're all just *hating me!*
I never *hated* back,
That's my mistake, you see
Now it's too late, you see
Trust me, just wait and see . . .

. . . Wait till I get my own back!

Samara Straker (17)
St Francis Xavier Sixth Form College, London

Being Bullied

Bullies - so mean and aggressive
They attack and torture people
Hatred is their favourite hobby
Why do they use violence among others?

They leave us scared and frightened
Knowing that there's nothing we can do
Bang! Punch! Ow!
The poor victim is left weeping.

Bullies . . . ! Who are they?
They make us feel lonely and empty
The thoughts going through their head are pitch-black darkness
That our stomachs are left feeling cold.

The poor victim is left in the hospital bed
With a fractured wrist and a bruised eye
The parents are crying, wondering, 'Who did this?'
Bullies - that's who they are!

Alison Kusi-Manu (11)
Sion Manning RC Girls' School, Ladbroke Grove

Will I Ever Make It?

I want to be an actress,
Act in films
Live the glamorous,
Life is beautiful.

But when I look at my life,
I see all the killing and death,
A child killed by a knife,
Life is sometimes sad.

I want to watch a film,
But it's the news,
A man has been shot in his own home,
Life is sometimes shocking.

I'm in my drama lesson
And we have to do a role play,
A woman has been beaten to death by her son.
Life is unsafe.

When I go home,
A car turns round the corner
And crashes into another car,
Life isn't perfect.

It could be me,
When will it be?
Today? Tomorrow?
Will I ever make it?

Courtney Mae Osborne (12)
Sion Manning RC Girls' School, Ladbroke Grove

Questions Of Life

What is the meaning of life?
What are we doing here?
Why are we made?
Why is the Earth made?
Why are we different from others?
Why have we got different magical mothers?
Are we here for a reason?
We have to live life
We have to breathe life
It's only our life
When death comes, we have to go
Leave in peace
We have to say farewell to families and friends
Our spirit will rise from underneath our grave
It will leave while everyone is crying, without a trace
No one will see it and neither will you
It will rise to Heaven
It will go to the afterlife
We cannot change this
It's the way of our timeline
The afterlife is as bright as the sun
Everything you ever wanted is here
From now on, it will be your world
No one knows how you get there
But your spirit flies there
It's a place of dreams and wonders
You will live a new life
All in peace, all in quiet
So . . . what is the meaning of life?

Sabina Yareshko (12)
Sion Manning RC Girls' School, Ladbroke Grove

When? What? How?

Will it be today?
Will it be tomorrow?
Will it be full of happiness
Or unhappy sorrow?

Will people jump for joy?
Will they drown in tears?
Will their worries double?
Will their worries be a fear?

Will many people die,
After living a life of Hell?
Or will they survive,
With an amazing story to tell?

Will they keep the weapons,
As a primary source?
If you ask me,
I would endorse.

Oh, when will it be?
I wonder all the nights,
When will it be the end,
Of all the wars and fights?

Abigail Leitao (11)
Sion Manning RC Girls' School, Ladbroke Grove

Bullying

I was in my room all alone
Had nowhere to stay
And nothing to do
A knock on the door
I ran away,
What shall I do?
I will die
But I wanted to stay alive.

I stood up
Not knowing what to do
Looking back at the door
I heard a roar.

Back and forth
Where did it come from?
When I looked back at the door
I saw a face
A face that I'd never seen before
What shall I do?

The noise was getting louder and louder
Every minute looking at the door
The face wasn't there.

Zhaklina Dana (11)
Sion Manning RC Girls' School, Ladbroke Grove

The Meaning Of Life

There is a crime upon this land,
Started by the criminal's hand,
He who took a soul,
Landed in a great big hole.

Graffiti on the walls,
With a long line of tools,
Needed for weapons,
That looks like lemons.

Alone at night,
Feeling the fright,
Scared to death,
About the dangerous sight.

Not knowing what will happen,
Not knowing when it will end,
But feeling the strain,
He was in a lot of pain.

Now that he's got arrested,
He has confessed,
Leaving him jailed,
Without getting bailed.

Down in his heart,
He is broken apart,
For what he had done,
He has not won.

Louisa Alo (12)
Sion Manning RC Girls' School, Ladbroke Grove

The Meaning Of Life

People are different,
In their own unique way,
We were all made different,
In the slightest, smallest ways.

We are on this Earth,
For what reason and why?
Who made us?
Or did we just fall from the sky?

What is our job in this world today?
Young people take exams
So they can get a job with good pay.

Yaasantewa Stevenson (12)
Sion Manning RC Girls' School, Ladbroke Grove

Gymnastics

G irls running around the gym
Y ou must warm up before you begin
M ovements very swift and neat
N ot forgetting to point your feet
A crobatics all around
S ometimes high above the ground
T rying to do flips and balances on the beam
I t's much harder than it seems
C hallenging yourself to a more complex skill
S o you give yourself an extra thrill.

Sharna Leuschner (12)
Sion Manning RC Girls' School, Ladbroke Grove

Wannabe Beyoncé

Wearing brown weave to fix my hair,
Doing the 'Ah, oh' dance without no care.
Waiting backstage, waiting to go on,
Finally, that's it, I hear my song.
I see Jay-Z back in the crowd,
He better not take my spotlight, I'm the one wearing the crown.
It's my night to shine, it's all my stage,
His show was yesterday, don't make me complain.
I finished the show without no drama,
Now I can come home and be more calmer.

But wait a second, I have to do a photo shoot . . .

Flash, flash, here, *flash, flash,* there,
Hope it's in Vogue or I don't care.
I can be mean; I can be a diva,
Where's my chair and where's my water?
But wait a minute, it was all just a dream,
Me, my mirror, my brush and a little scream.

Michelle Aluko (12)
Sion Manning RC Girls' School, Ladbroke Grove

Gun Crime

There I stood, all alone,
In the black darkness,
With my phone.

I dialled her number
And hoped for an answer,
But there was no one to answer,
As I stood there alone,
I knelt down and cried.

'Why me?' I asked,
I heard a sound
Laughter
I looked around,
Shivered.

The sound was coming closer
I heard a shot burst into the air
I tried to make myself small
Like a balloon.

Another shot fired into the air
I put my hand on my heart
As I sunk into the ground
And was out of bound.

Nicole Busz (11)
Sion Manning RC Girls' School, Ladbroke Grove

Scared!

If you are scared of puberty,
You must be scared of poverty,
With all the things on your mind,
You must be scared of pregnancy,
As you must know drugs are a crime,

That's the whole point of why I'm doing this rhyme!

While gangs are getting bigger,
More are pulling the trigger,
While lives are getting shorter,
Toddlers are growing faster,
If you think you can do the time,
Go ahead and do the crime,

Life is not long, so you've got to stay strong,

Live your life day by day
And please, don't go astray!

Soumia Dehbi (11)
Stockwell Park High School, London

The Beginning Of The End!

M y generation
Y our short life

G uns will end it before your time
E ducation gets lower
N egativity gets higher
E verything you worked for is hanging on a wire
R egenerate the peace
A nd be so free
T omorrow you will live to turn over a new leaf
I n the real world, it's only one opportunity
O nly one glance
N ow know what you are.

Ismael Turay (12)
Stockwell Park High School, London

What I Turned Into

The day I never got a job, I felt ugly,
People stared and said I'm a crackhead
I chase children, because I have nothing to do
I rob the shop near me to get scollsuper
I call myself Diggy-Diggy,
I sit around because there is nothing to do
And my hair looks like doo-doo
I go to McDonald's and ask for some food
But all they say is, 'Blah, blah, blah'
When it rains, I have nowhere to go
But people say I'm blocking the way.

When people look at me they laugh
But I look to myself and say
If only I did better, I would not be in this mess.

Natasha Thiel & Giselle Dacruz Routledge (12)
Stockwell Park High School, London

What Is The World Coming To?

All this shooting, there's no need
Just for a stupid little bag of weed.
Prostitution, poverty, we've had enough,
All we need is a little bit of love.

Racism, racism, black against white,
All this nonsense ending in a fight.
All these areas making gangs
Giving random people straight one, two bangs.

All these people getting into trouble
Getting into trouble, then getting in a rumble.
Friends and family dying every day
And relatives sit in rooms and pray.

Ramone Edwards (12)
Stockwell Park High School, London

School Days

Here I am, at school once again
Hoping for the day to fly away
Seeing people being bullied
Seeing people being silly

I'm doing lessons that are never fun
But one more day and it will come
I'll be on holiday doing what I enjoy
Playing on the beach, like a normal boy

No more school
No more rules
No more schoolwork
No more homework

I love the sun shining in my face
Making me feel free to all the pain
But one thing makes me go insane
I'm back at school, once again.

Albere Lisbie (11)
Stockwell Park High School, London

My Heart Is Here For Me!

My heart is a singing bird
    Whose nest is in a watered shoot
My heart is like an apple tree
    Whose boughs are bent with sweetened fruit.

My heart is like a rainbow
    It paddles in an ocean sea
My heart is like a red rose
    Because my love is here for me.

Simone Kimone King (13)
Stockwell Park High School, London

My Sister, Raesher

My sister, Raesher, she is so cute
Her face is as soft as a tulip
She has a lovely smile
Her smile is as big as an ocean
And her eyes are as bright as a shining star
Sometimes she's annoying
She creeps up on you like a creepy spider
She roars with her gigantic voice
Then suddenly, she smiles and smiles and smiles
My sister, Raesher, she eats like a pig
My mum gives her a hot bottle of milk
And she stuffs it down her throat which makes her choke
I wonder if she's really my sister, I ask in a whisper
Although she's a whimper, I still love her.

Kimberlee Noble (13)
Stockwell Park High School, London

My Life

I might be young, but I am stressing
When I am older
Don't want to keep looking over shoulders
When I mean shoulder, yes, I mean mine
It's just a matter of time
Before I go to college and learn a new trade
Want to be successful and big in the game
When I go to work, I am not taking the train
I am going to be driving my car
Through London people, going to say 'rah
Another black boy that made it so far
It's not a racial thing, so I'm not being rude
Want to settle down, want a relationship
Don't want to use slang words, like 'gash', 'neek' or 'prick'
All I need is education and that is it!

Evan Edwards (12)
Stockwell Park High School, London

Oh No! What Am I Going To Do?

Oh no! I've made a big mistake!
What am I going to do?
I've gone and got myself pregnant!
What am I going to do?
I don't know who the father is,
It's a choice between the two!

I needed the money!
It's not my fault,
Each second I think about the day I'll get caught!
What would my parents do to me?
No day after that I will see!
Oh my gosh! They might kill me!

I wish this was just all a dream!
In the night you can hear me scream!
What am I going to do?
What am I going to do?

Charlie Read (12)
Stockwell Park High School, London

What Happens On The Streets

Gun crime is happening a lot of the time
It is horrible, I know, but the flowers still show
Mums are losing kids and dogs being trained to fight
You can hear them howling through the night.

People being mugged for their money and phones
They tell you to keep quiet or they'll raid your homes
They hang out on the streets, just talking and dealing
Sometimes I wonder what they're feeling.

They beat you up and they leave you in the street
Be careful of the people that you meet
Police are catching them, while they're painting their mark
Sometimes you find them in the park.

If they catch you, do not shiver
That encourages them to pull the trigger
Some carry guns and some carry knives
And some think that they have great lives.

Jamie Gale (11)
Stockwell Park High School, London

Gangs Do Violent Crimes

Gangs do violent crimes,
Gangs carry weapons and do violent crimes,
Bang! The gang carry big guns
Slang, the gang talks when they dig for fun,
Gangs think they are strong when they're with friends,
Gangs long for strong members when they are weak.

Police chase to get rid of banging,
But gangs keep on running in sight of the police,
Gangs go in groups of people and rob,
Although they sob in front of their parents,
The gangs in truth, are scared,
They bang and fight,
Most of them say rude words, thinking they are bad,
Costly of 'em to brag about that when they are sad.

Alone and away at alleyways,
Gangs go and ambush people alone,
Gangs are extremely dangerous,
When dogs are following,
Gangsters bang other gangs and fight,
They fight like they're the best.

In the faraway end,
The cars are around the bend,
The gangs test gangsters by sending 'em,
In the bitter truth of the dark ways,
The dogs bark and say *woof*
Sitting down the hole
Sucking up the whole truth.

James Chu (12)
Stockwell Park High School, London

How Depressing Life Is!

Miserable child looking for happiness,
Looking for his lost souls,
Brother and cousin, friends all gone,
Which is hurting the child inside,
Weeping in the heart,
Laughing on the outside, acting like nothing is wrong,
Wanting attention, which he cannot get,
Searching for the right things and company,
Looking for a better life, trying to get out of gangs,
Need the lost souls for everything to be alright,
Going cemetary laying down roses and taking pictures
And going to sing a prayer to keep him strong
And think about the family,
Getting weaker inside,
Hearts now breaking, searching for someone
To hold him when he falls,
Looking for someone to pick up the pieces,
Starts to weep, heart's now aching,
He opens his eyes, tears run down his cheeks,
Depressed, young man searching for someone to hold,
From 11 to 13, all this has happened.

Malakai Campbell (12)
Stockwell Park High School, London

War Poem

War, war, war
All I can see is people dying,
All I can hear is people whining,
People talking, people walking,
Sounds of those talking.

Sounds of death awaiting,
Machines, trucks, guns and bombs,
The cries of the desperate men,
Thinking, *am I going to die today*
Or am I going to live another day?

Cries all about,
Of people that are dead and people lost,
Bodies falling down to the ground,
People losing all the pounds,
Body parts being scattered,
All their hair matted.

People helping those wounded,
People helping those injured,
Guns lying on the ground,
Losing all the pounds,
War, war, war!

Jade Carrington
The Matthew Arnold School, Staines

Sadness

Sadness is as bad as an evil witch,
Sadness is as cold as a wintry night.
Sadness is despair hope,
Sadness is failing your exams.
Here comes sadness, wearing a black hoodie,
Sad face, baggy pants and has no friends,
Are you often sad?

Aarthi Adimulam (12)
The Matthew Arnold School, Staines

War

Frightened soldiers in their line
Waiting for the battle time
Knowing that death is on his way
Hoping they'll live another day
Gunshots, screams and wailing men
Wishing to see dead friends again
Bodies, tanks and blood-stained floors
What could possibly be gained from war?

Injured bodies strewn across the ground
Orders, shrieks and groaning sounds
Soldiers as blue as a cloudless sky
Innocent men, left to die
War is angry, loud and mean
War is a killing machine
War is sad, war is bad, war is mad
It will not make you glad.

Tasmin Arnould (13)
The Matthew Arnold School, Staines

War

War is as big as Earth
And there will be no birth.
My legs are killing me to death
And my arms are left alone.
The rapid fire burns my heart,
A part of my heart bleeds to death.
Oh please, oh please,
Can you save me
From this mess?
My little belly rumbles and grumbles
And looks like a bubble.
I can smell the delicious, tasty buns to eat
And we always get beat.
We see the big, fat, lovely buns to eat,
But we need a seat to eat.

Daniel Choi
The Matthew Arnold School, Staines

War Poem

'Open fire! Open fire!'
That's what you hear the general shout;
Over the top, it smells of human waste
Drop dead Fred, it's OK.

Blood splattered everywhere
I miss my kids and the baker
Reload the guns before the attack,

Help the wounded, you don't even know them,
You're all there to settle this.

Cries of men.

Bodies and parts on the floor -
Ow! Cuts and bruises;
It's all souvenirs from the war.

You get back, but not everyone is there -
You just look around and stare,
You're happy to see your family,
But the baker is not there.

But not everyone's family is happy.

Joseph Burgess
The Matthew Arnold School, Staines

Sadness

Sadness comes, sadness goes
It's cold, it rolls, it bowls round your head
Makes you sad when it's inside you
Makes you cold when it's beside you
Take the tablet, one, two, three:
Make happiness for you and me.

Rhys Parker
The Matthew Arnold School, Staines

Friendship

Without our friends
Life would be boring,
We meet our friends
In the morning,
Don't be alone
Or you will just
Moan, moan, moan.

At school, we have a laugh
My friends are all a bit daft,
If my friends weren't there
I would not laugh every minute
Of every year.

My friends are like family,
At the weekend, I go
Out with my mates,
I am never late,
Because of my mates.

Rianne Hicks (13)
The Matthew Arnold School, Staines

War

When the day is done, another has just begun,
Fighting for one's country
And becoming more and more and numb.

War has set a blanket,
Across the shining blue sky,
The blanket that hides
The happiness we need to get by.

Slowly, numbers go down in their thousands,
Each day, more and more die,
The horrible sight of chaos
And the sounds of the soldiers' cry.

Rebecca Sedgwick
The Matthew Arnold School, Staines

The Forgotten City

Deep below the city streets, lurks a place long forgotten
In this place, stands a solitary figure,
Cast astray from society,
Chosen not to be acknowledged.
Yet, his mind does not stray,
He is focused on the task ahead of him,
He remains concentrated on his routine,
Which engulfs his life.

The tunnel shakes, as a train passes by,
His mind wanders for a moment,
Of life outside his sewers.
Refocused, he continues his repetitive work,
Unappreciated by the world above.

Jack Yates (14)
The Matthew Arnold School, Staines

Sadness

Sadness is an emotion
We all feel in our lifetime:
We can be crying inside
But our faces will be dry.
There will be no tears
Sadness is alive, standing in
A puddle of water, crying.
I trip over to a journey out of
Happiness and into sadness
And I hurt my knee and it's
Paining me.
Where once I felt nothing; now
Something.

Why is this world steeped in so much sadness?

Grant Williams-Nicholson (12)
The Matthew Arnold School, Staines

Secret Garden

Tweet, tweet
Here and there,
Plants to my left,
Plants to my right,
Pretty colours,
Blues and oranges,
Greens and yellows,
I'm surrounded and yet, I'm all alone.

People passing, in a rush,
So unaware of my quiet little place,
They don't know what they're missing!
It's good though, I suppose,
My own little safe haven - a secret!
A break from the routine - the normality!
This place is my salvation.

Mary Symons (14)
The Matthew Arnold School, Staines

Holiday Parrot

I arrived at my destination
Camden Town
A rough landing
Fell . . . the canal

People weren't that friendly
Looking grumpy
Colourful hair
Blue, red, green
Like my feathers - bright
Smoking and drinking
Dirty streets

I was scared
It turned dark
Riots and police
I want my mummy
Busy, noisy, loud
Flashing lights
Crowding fights

Back home
Calm and quiet
Worst holiday . . . ever
Never go back there
Without Mummy and Daddy.

Dannielle Rose (12)
The Royal Free Hospital Children's School, London

The Rhyming Generation

I look around and there's no doubt,
I know my time is running out.
I want to change the world around,
But speaking out is only the sound.

Youth is like a blossoming flower,
I should be kept safe and sound.
But think about how much a flower
Actually moves around.

Compare myself to a flower,
It is a bit like me.
Very well looked after,
But never really free.

They say I need tranquillity,
In my youthful vulnerability.
Because of this I'll never know,
How far I could really go.

I run like clockwork, in perfect time,
Like this poem in rhythmic rhyme.
Does every syllable have to fit?
Can I not break free a bit?

Elsa Vulliamy (13)
The Royal Free Hospital Children's School, London

My Generation

Life comes with a package
Sometimes it makes you cry
And sometimes it makes you smile
It has never been the same
The seasons have come and gone
But the vision of teenagers hasn't changed
We teenagers, all irresponsible, blunt and careless
Though our parents were the same.
But look back
They were full of culture and traditions
Had respect for others
And wouldn't ruin their parent's dream
They are our role model
But here we are
Thinking about ourselves and our needs
So where do our parent's dreams fit in?
They aren't selfish
They have been through a lot
Fulfilling their dreams
That's the only aim we should have.

Tamkinat Ijaz (17)
Uxbridge College, Uxbridge

My Generation

We are the world's children and the generation,
Who should be making things better for the future,
Less fortunate kids in Third World countries want to learn,
Instead we play truant and throw away our education.

Things are not how they used to be,
Our childhood is only for a short while,
So make the most of it,
When are we going to open our eyes and see?

Teenagers are often portrayed as rebellious,
Do we have to live up to this name?
Having sex, doing drugs and making quick money,
Has become our essential aim.

The media has brainwashed our generation,
To believe this is the life we should lead,
From what I have seen,
It looks like we are all in turmoil.

Some perceive life as a game,
Well, the ball is in our courts,
So how do you want to play?

Sherise Charlotte Fletcher (17)
Uxbridge College, Uxbridge

My Generation

A generation of a good generation
Where I am growing from one day
My generation will come and they will
Be inspired by inspiration.

Never know what tomorrow lies
Make generation good today and it will
Come in future, better
Although people think my generation is bad
But I know there's a lot of inspiration.

Generation comes and goes
Set a good background for the next
Generation, because what goes around
Comes around.

My generation is good
A background has been set.

It's my turn to reach that because
The inspiration is there
The sky is my limit, there is no
Stopping point; just keep flying
So that the next generation would
Also set a good background.

A place full of inspiration, there are
Doctors, lawyers, engineers and nurses.

It's my turn to show what I can do
What my generation today is
And what I can be for another
Generation in future.

Charles Jackson **(17)**
Uxbridge College, Uxbridge

My Generation

Take a moment to think about my generation
I can guess what you imagine

Young girls on the streets
Vomiting after their latest session of underage drinking

Gangs hanging out in parks and alleys
Shouting abuse at all those near
Destroying anything in their path

Single, teenage mums in council flats
Living off the state
Surrounded by children they can't afford

This is the image portrayed by the media
A generation of useless layabouts
Too lazy to work, expecting everything handed to them

This is not what I see
I see a generation tolerant and accepting of those around them
Free from prejudice

I see a generation aware of the effect on the world
A world they wish to make better

I see a generation pressured to achieve perfection
To achieve the dreams of the generations before them

We live in a media-obsessed society
Watching every action of so-called celebrities

In a flawed society, we are a generation
Tarnished by the actions of a minority

So, I ask you, do not judge us by our age or our peers
We're all individual.

Naomi Haysum (16)
Uxbridge College, Uxbridge

My Generation

Let me tell you 'bout my generation
A generation with complications
And we seem to get ourselves in bad situations
From England to the surrounding nations
Entering the country by means of immigration
Actually no, not my generation
My generation's bad, that's a dumb exaggeration
People just wanna talk with no hesitation.

People say we're just about guns and knives
But not me, I'm not really 'bout guns and knives
Cos I know people who wanna do something with their lives
Achieve that legal money without a knife
Just thinking about that million will make some wanna strive
Get good grades in school, or no point living my *life*
Cos we can listen to music and get into the *vibes*
And the opposite sex, treat fairly and be faithful to our wives.

Dylan Donald (16)
Uxbridge College, Uxbridge

My Generation

Generation, what can I say?

Life is tough for us youths
We have family, school, work
Including the home
Yes, it can be joyful at times
But joy isn't enough for us at times

Generation today, what can I say?

Life on the roads, friends, including enemies
One person saying, 'wagwan' to another
It's all 'bless'
It's all about making money
But *some* in the wrong way!
Thieving, selling, whatever helps my generation get by.

Generation today, what can I say?

Alkesh Solanki (17)
Uxbridge College, Uxbridge

My Generation

The world runs,
Runs in different generations!

Humans, animals and the nature,
Live in the world,
See how the world changes.

My generation,
Where nothing's left, except
Hate, selfishness, crime and sadness.

People sometimes behaving like animals
Bad body language and speaking attitude.

My generation contains laziness
Machines and computers made us humans lazy
People don't do their work by nature.

What will happen in the next generation?
In the next generation,
Where everything will be electronic
And no nature will be left, no nature!

Suri Sonam (17)
Uxbridge College, Uxbridge

My Generation

Today's society people aren't aware of the lack of prosperity
Children running the streets at the age of ten
Causing havoc, committing crime
Today they're called hoodlums
Selling drugs from weed to speed to crack cocaine
All those youths thinking it'll free their pain
Unaware of the dangers and the long-term effect
I just don't understand why this generation has no respect?
Nine teenagers killed so far this year
As a result, the rest of us walk around in fear
Giving us an easier excuse to carry a weapon
Half of those kids are living a life of deception
Doing it for fun, hooligans on the run
So beware when you walk around a corner
Because you might just be next for the slaughter.

Jessica Price (17)
Uxbridge College, Uxbridge

My Generation

My generation,
Have no respect for our nation,
It's all about our style,
Old people say it's vile.

Most of all our money,
Is spent on Nikes, not honey,
We never earn our keep,
We just ride in our dad's Jeep.

We hardly ever care,
For paying the bus fare,
We sneak in through the back,
Not a thought of the Union Jack.

To summarise a point,
Before I go to a burger joint,
We care more about football,
Than going to a book stall!

Kulvinder Nagre (11)
William Ellis School, London

My Generation

My generation's the place to be
You can come and go whenever you please
From country to country
To planet to planet
Come on, my generation's the place to be
Life is easy, life is fun, life is the best it's ever been
You can do this, you can do that
Make a call on the loo
Type up your homework in ten minutes max
My generation's the place to be
The place where you can do all these.

Quinton Huntesmith (11)
William Ellis School, London

My Generation

M obile phones, mp3 players, memory sticks
Y ou would think that you could take your pick

G ordon Brown, global warming, game consoles
E veryone wants more fun and less homework
N ot everyone in this world has all these gadgets
E verything is always changing
R unning seems to be what everyone is doing
A nimals are endangered and some are extinct
T he fast food is getting people fatter
I think this world is too full of cars
O lympics is in China this year
N othing is normal and everything is different.

Andrew Green (11)
William Ellis School, London

My Generation

M y generation
Y ears of not caring about our nation

G reatness just going to waste
E ngland is just about having good taste
N obody cares about our planet
E veryone's searching for their hidden talent
R ushing around for nothing but money
A busing life like it's something funny
T raditions are just going down the drain
I t's leaving all the old people in so much pain
O ver-taxing like it's just a game
N o one cares about anything but fame.

Lucas Attwood (12)
William Ellis School, London

Young Writers Information

We hope you have enjoyed reading this book - and that you will continue to enjoy it in the coming years.

If you like reading and writing poetry drop us a line, or give us a call, and we'll send you a free information pack.

Alternatively if you would like to order further copies of this book or any of our other titles, then please give us a call or log onto our website at www.youngwriters.co.uk

Young Writers Information
Remus House
Coltsfoot Drive
Peterborough
PE2 9JX
(01733) 890066